A Sunny Subaltern

BILLY'S LETTERS FROM FLANDERS

McCLELLAND, GOODCHILD & STEWART
PUBLISHERS : : : : TORONTO

COPYRIGHT, CANADA, 1916.
BY McCLELLAND, GOODCHILD & STEWART, LIMITED,
TORONTO.

PRINTED IN CANADA.

Printing Statement:

Due to the very old age and scarcity of this book, many of the pages may be hard to read due to the blurring of the original text, possible missing pages, missing text, dark backgrounds and other issues beyond our control.

Because this is such an important and rare work, we believe it is best to reproduce this book regardless of its original condition.

Thank you for your understanding.

RESPECTFULLY DEDICATED TO
THE BRAVE OFFICERS AND MEN
OF "BILLY'S" BATTALION.

PREFACE

At the earnest solicitation of friends I am publishing these letters, which were written without any attempt at literary effect and intended only for a mother's eye. I am sure my son will be pleased if they are the means of bringing even a passing pleasure to those whose dear ones are now at the front, to those whose loved ones have made the supreme sacrifice, and to any others who may read this book. This be my apology for offering them to the public.

"BILLY'S" MOTHER.

A Sunny Subaltern

November 23, 1915.

Well, the great adventure is on. We sailed out of St. John at noon to-day amid a perfect babel of noise. We have on board with us the ——, a detail of Medical Corps, the ——, and a detail of the Construction Corps, —— troops in all. Between the bands of the units, the bands in St. John, the shrieks of what seemed a thousand tugs which bobbed beside —— "a regular bedlam" best describes the send off. Every pier looked as if it had been generously salted and peppered from one end of the harbour to the last long dock; I say salted and peppered, for the sea of faces and dark clothes gave it that appearance. Well, anyway, away we steamed out into the East.

A SUNNY SUBALTERN

I can assure you, Mother, I felt rather proud of being in khaki as we marched through the thronged streets. The bands playing martial airs seemed to send little shivers up and down my spine, and, I guess, awoke some of the old primordial instinct of the cave man for it sure seemed glorious to be on the way to fight. I know you dear ones would have been proud, too, of me and the men. I say the men, for after all Tommy is the most important man in the Army and our whole battalion behaved like nature's gentlemen in St. John. However, out we steamed on a sea like an epergne base—not a ripple hardly. Of course we didn't have much time but I managed to stand about four p.m. and watch the last grey humps of Canada fade into the waves, my last glimpse of my native land for some time to come, and do you know, dear, that despite the fact that there lay all my associations, my love and everything that any man holds dear, I can't say I was sorry, for ahead there is something that dwarfs all those details.

11.30 p.m.—Have just passed Cape Sable light house, the last link with land, flashing in and out of the night. A beautiful night, clear moonlit water, and just enough breeze to send a salt spray up over the bows.

Wednesday Evening.—Nothing new to-day. The ocean like a mill pond all day and not even a roll to this old packet. We have a few men who are seasick, but I think they must be awfully upset with something for it's smoother than Lake Ontario.

Later.—I have just taken a turn on deck and the wind is getting up, also the sea, and a small look at the barometer informs me she is at 29. The 1st Officer says it looks like a storm, so I fear me there is dirty work aboard the lugger this evening.

A SUNNY SUBALTERN

Friday Evening.—This discrepancy is due, not to sea sickness, but to the fact that I was on guard from 10 a.m. yesterday till 10 a.m. to-day, and in about as bad weather as I really care ever to see. It started in Wednesday night and blew a regular gale head on, for thirty-six hours. There is no use in my trying to describe it for I can't. Suffice it to say she was a real storm. My clothes are not dry yet, being soaked through and through. Everyone was seasick, and if I could describe the indescribable horror of men crowded together as they were in those days, I know you wouldn't believe me. Oh! it was horrible. Sick by hundreds lying around anywhere gasping for air. Some slept on the decks in a drenched condition, spray sweeping over them, and of thirty-nine men on guard I finished up with nine, the remainder all being sick. The stench below was something to remember, and oh, how I longed to take some of the men up into our comfortable quarters. I was up for practically twenty-four hours and on deck two out of every six hours most of the time, except when making rounds on the bridge, and my descriptive vocabulary fails me when I try to tell you what the tail end of it was like early this morning. We have a slight list to port—coal moved, probably—and she heaved and plunged like a broncho in the huge waves that drenched me clear up on the bridge. One man of the crew was killed, washed off the ladder leading to the crow's nest into the forward winches. Broken neck. He was buried this a.m. However, it has quieted down now and to-night is smooth again.

Saturday Night.—By the way I forgot to mention that I must be an A1 sailor, for nearly every one has been ill but myself. I have eaten every meal and enjoyed them and never felt the slightest squeam-

A SUNNY SUBALTERN

ishness, even at meals, despite the fact that "the Captains and Colonels departed" (apologies to Rud) from the table very hurriedly at times. There is no news worthy of mention. We are again on a sea of glass and it has been bright and warm, in fact warmer than I've felt for two months, and we're in mid-Atlantic. To-night it is like Summer, and others who have crossed before say it is colder in July than this trip. Just at present we are cleaving our way into a road of silver, for the moon is shining directly over our bows, and it is a wonderful sight apparently moving up a shimmering carpet right to the old man of green cheese fame. At least that is the impression recorded by me. A carpet of silver and grey lace, like one of those red and black ones from the sidewalk to a church door at weddings, dancing ahead and only the lap, lap, lap of the waters as one stands on the fo'castle.

A SUNNY SUBALTERN

Monday Evening.—Nothing very new, my dear, to write, just the old monotony of the voyage, which, when it ends will be a relief. The sea has changed, and from a head on affair has turned about and we get her abeam! result, a roll in place of a pitch. We are beginning to get into the war zone more than before, and expect on Tuesday and Wednesday to be near it if not right in it.

Wednesday Morning.—Yesterday we had a parade with life belts on, every man on board and also life-boat drill. It is really our first taste of what is sure to come later, that is, having to calmly face the possibility of death, and do you know it really didn't seem to bother me at all. I suppose the thoughts of it for months and months have somewhat dulled and sensibilities of "yours truly."

To-morrow we expect to be in ———.

BILLY.

IN CAMP, ENGLAND,
December 5, 1915.

Dear Mother,—

As you will see, we are here. Since sending the sort of diary I wrote on board boat, we have simply arrived and come here. As we came up the channel in the grey of the morning it surely looked good to see land and the cliffs of Land's End and Cornwall. The whole channel was dotted with small steam trawlers used as mine sweepers, and then after we passed The Lizard, and our signals were taken from the shore station, out of the distance came six torpedo boat destroyers tearing along at forty miles an hour and surrounded us. Ahead, just over the horizon, steamed a huge cruiser. Well, anyway, just after lunch we steamed into Plymouth harbour, a rare old spot indeed, filled with historic memories and its history checkered with incidents. Devonport beside it

A SUNNY SUBALTERN

is a huge naval dockyard, and revenue cutters and naval tugs with tenders soon surrounded us and our baggage, etc., was removed to shore. As it was very late at night when we arrived we remained on board all night and started off at 9 a.m.

Two naval tugs named after two Plymouth heroes, Raleigh and Drake, conveyed us to shore. Between frowning walls of grey stone, with here and there guns nosing their way out, we landed on a quay and entrained in a long English train. At eleven we started, arriving at 8 p.m., but just to dissect my feelings or to describe to you the journey, is a task I can scarcely begin. You know everything was so different that my head fairly ached from madly turning from one side of the coach to the other in a vain endeavour to see everything from barmaids to ruined castles, my first glimpse of either. The quaint old churches with their tiny graveyards; the infinitesimal quadrangles of yellow, black, and red, called fields; the moss-covered banks and ivy-clad houses; the oaks festooned with ivy, mistletoe and holly all in red and white bloom; the villages and towns all the same, checkerboards of roofs with houses identical as if they had been turned out of a machine; the shapely hedgerows; the quiet looking sheep, and wild-eyed cattle; the rabbits scurrying at the train; the pheasants in hundreds, with here and there a heron guarding a tiny pool; the funny little stations, yellow, exactly like the ones in toy train sets, the white lines between green ones signifying a road—all these are jumbled up in my mind into a hodge podge of pictures that is so conglomerate I fear me it will take some time to sort them out. Of one thing I am certain, however, that England is exactly as described in anything I ever read and it fully "lives up to its picture

A SUNNY SUBALTERN

book reputation." I little wonder that England has produced Chaucer, Milton, Shakespeare, Dickens, and after looking at a grey and ivied church with its old belfry and the funny grey slabs, some aslant, some flat, some erect in the iron-palinged graveyard, I can realize how the Elegy was inspired.

Well, we arrived at a depot at 8 p.m., pitch dark, and were met by staff officers, who escorted us here about four miles. This is under the famous Aldershot command which has 200,000 troops in it and there are several camps. We are the first battalion of "Canadians," as we are called, to be here, and the other units turned out, and cheer after cheer went up as we marched in. There is a Brigade of the Royal Sussex, the Middlesex; then regiments of Argyll and Sutherland Highlanders, Irish Fusiliers, Gloucester and others, all famous English corps. There are twenty odd thousand in this camp

A SUNNY SUBALTERN

with room for seventy. Each platoon has a long building to itself and every convenience that one could imagine. Water, hot and cold baths, electric lights, game rooms, large, bright, airy mess rooms, concrete walks everywhere—in fact it is a revelation.

We officers have splendid quarters. A large house for mess with huts of eight rooms, four to a room, at rear a fire place tiled in each room, and bath attached, so we are not too bad.

However, if I tell all the news at once I won't have anything to write for next time, so will close. With fondest love to all.

BILLY.

Have just remembered you will get this about Christmas, so will wish you all a very Merry Christmas and Happy New Year. That's all I can send you just now, but when I get up to London will send something more tangible, but you understand my position. There are no stores here.

IN CAMP.
December 14, 1915.

Dear Mother,—

Received the letter you wrote addressed to Army P.O., but have mislaid it for the time, so cannot name date. However, as I want to catch the Canadian mail will just ramble on.

Since I last wrote you I've had so many impressions etched on my brain that it will be a very incoherent affair, this letter. You know everything is so totally foreign to the style of life I've been accustomed to that it is staggering. However, my impressions, muddled as they seem, may make reading. Ever since childhood I have studied opposites, and I suppose that one of the first impressions a child gets is light and dark, after that heat and cold, and its about these latter I wish to write. The cold over

A SUNNY SUBALTERN

here is a very good cold that is true to type. It is cold and goes clean through, and the heat differentiates from any heat which heretofore has caused my corpuscles to quicken, by doing the exact opposite of the cold, viz., it fails to penetrate. I am convinced that if there was enough of it, it would be jake, but the great aim and object of the nation here seems to be to heat the chimney. At a time when the slogan is, "Conserve the national resources," they are per second shooting sufficient calories of heat out into the wide world (through chimney pots) to make Hades an air-cooled six-cylinder self-starter, and Satan to resign. Their grates are pretty, but as purveyors of warmth where needed fail to suit "yours trooly." This is at least one of the most vivid impressions I have and a poignant regret as well. That much for the knock. Now for some boosts. She surely is a *land* and as I told you measures up in scenic investiture better than any scenic artist's stage production ever could hope to.

Last Wednesday we took part in Brigade manoeuvres with the 117th Brigade of the English Army doing about eighteen miles' march. It was the first day in which Old Sol deigned to lighten his lamp for us and a beautiful day for marching. Between miles of hedges, along roads like pavement, by tiny rivers, over quaint bridges, through hamlets with typical inns as laid out by Dickens & Co. and by a Smithy shop under a chestnut tree that might have been the one Longfellow wrote about. The hedges complied with all regulations, draped in fall grandeur, punctuated here and there by a red exclamation mark in the form of a holly bush and from which at intervals scampered a sleek looking grey hare or else flew up a scared pheasant. Anyway it was a day I will long remember,

A SUNNY SUBALTERN

one in which picture after picture was limned on my memory in indelible colours.

It was a great sight, too, to see with glasses from a hill all the troops in action: cavalry, artillery, infantry, signallers, cyclists and a large squad of aeroplanes which glinted and dipped here and there in the sunlight. We arrived back at 6 p.m. tired, but I sure had enough thoughts to keep me thinking, also wishing you could have been with me to enjoy all the grandeur of it. Picturesque Surrey surely lives up to its reputation.

Saturday most of the boys went to London, but Young, two others and myself went to Guilford, some fourteen miles. It is a quaint old town modernized. Here it was that Henry VIII. murdered Anne Boleyn, if you remember history, and I saw an old Grammar school authorized in 1555 by Edward VI.

and still intact, as well as other old buildings. We went over by taxi. I had some purchases to make and I can assure you that a £ doesn't go as far here as a V at home; as near as I can figure everything is seven and six. It seems to me a sort of national fetish, either five and six or seven and six, and I may add that your loving son was short changed for somewhere near $2 as well as I can figure. Of course this is a general thing and anybody with a maple leaf is game with no close season, so being prepared in a measure I am sorer than ever. A dimpled dame with a smile like Calypso, a voice like Circe's pipe and a complexion *a la* Mrs. Gervais Graham, while selling me a nail brush, eased the harpoon into me so neatly that I never felt $2 worth of barb till some time after when my numbed senses limbered into action. It sure beats all how easy one is, and I always figured I was no simp; but Barnum was right.

As I say, seven and six seems to be a fetish. At least everything that one wanted figured out at that price, except a pair of gloves which I could buy in Canada for $1.75—here they ask only eighteen shillings! Somewhere I had a vague idea that gloves were cheap over here. Say not so.

There was, however, a marketable commodity known as dinner, which we purchased at a "Recommended Hostelry" and which was only six shillings and three pence. Wouldn't that cause your grey locks to curl? $1.52 for a second class meal in a third rate tavern served in eighth class style; but oh, as a recompense I had an opportunity of studying in her native haunts Ye Barmaid. A ravishing blonde type, evidently belonging to the Amazonian family, nearly always found in rear of polished mahogany raking her lair of crystals and towels. Habits affable, courteous, quick and usually gifted with a line of repartee totally foreign to any other species. So you see there was a rose to the thorn even tho' the stab was a little deep. I may also add that I was introduced to Mr. Brown's October Ale, and found that he is some kicker. At least he has much more kick than his cousin Bud. In fact Bud may be wiser but not nearly as strong. Well, dears, there is very little more to tell except that with the exception of one day it has rained almost continually.

Love to —— and all the family, also remember me to anyone who cares.

BILLY.

December 20, 1915.

Dear Mother,—

Another week gone by and to catch the Canadian mail must write to-night. I've only had one letter from you since I came and no picture of you, Maw; perhaps it has gone astray. However, I'll let you know later.

To begin the chronicle of the week: It's just the same old story, so many vivid colours on my brain I cannot seem to start. However, I am taking a course in physical and bayonet fighting. It's all courses over here: musketry, bombing, artillery, entrenching or my own it seems—half of the Lieutenants are at one or the other. Mine is Swedish exercises. A wiry little Englishman puts us through (two hours in the morning and two in the afternoon) the toughest kind of physical drill, crashing hither and thither until I sometimes wonder if I'm a bird or only a relative of the nimble chamois which I am told leaps from crag to crag. At any rate I've been stiff and sore ever since I started, in fact there are a lot of muscles in my carcass that I never even suspected, and after four hours I say with fervour "Straafe Sweden." We start soon to give it to the companies, and believe me I'll get some action then.

Something that made a profound impression on me was a big service here yesterday, 5,000 men with four bands all in a little glen. Can you imagine 5,000 throats pealing out "O Come all Ye Faithful" and "Onward Christian Soldiers" to the accompaniment of 150 instruments. It echoed and reverberated I'm sure for miles, and in the midst of all the khaki one lone figure in a cassock of white and black. If you could close your eyes and see it as I do, I know you'd appreciate it.

Well, I saw London, only a sort of moving picture but nevertheless *London*. Yesterday—Sunday—was a glorious fall day, sunlit and warm, so as there were very few staying in camp six of us decided to go up to the city. We left at 12.05 p.m. and arrived back 11.30 p.m. Of course I couldn't tell you much about the place; it is just a confused jumble of gray stone buildings and rattling taxis; of khaki, khaki everywhere, always attached to a woman; of narrow sidewalks and crowded hotels; of old rose and gold restaurants mirrored all around and reflecting principally gorgeously gowned women all sipping tea and smoking cigarettes; of varied smells from sewers and cheap perfume to roses; of rumbling motor busses with, sticking out prominently, Trafalgar Square; service in Westminster with a golden throated choir; of women, women, women, in fact, never knew there were so many; of dark streets at night; of the Thames by moonlight; and oh! a thousand and one other views all hashed up. I think the real things that stand out are the innumerable women, apparently all smoking cigarettes, and the price of dinner at the Cecil which I'm not going to tell you as your frugal mind would do a flivver I'm sure.

A SUNNY SUBALTERN

But as I remarked before, they get enough over here. Of course you say "Why go there?" but there are only certain places officers are permitted to go, practically no restaurants outside the Criterion, Trocadero and the Cecil and Savoy, outside Claridge's and some of the high-priced hotels. But anyway I enjoyed the fleeting trip and expect to spend six days there when I get my leave, and of course I want then to see the sights that are worth seeing, not just the hustle and bustle.

Well, there is nothing really more to tell. We just go on each day with the usual work. Last Friday was out again with the Brigade with blank ammunition machine guns and real shells in artillery. We did good work and got the decision over the four other battalions.

I think you had better address the mail c/o Army P.O. as we may move from here to some other camp.

A SUNNY SUBALTERN

I suppose that over there now it's cold and lots of snow while here everything is green. So different, and sometimes I grow just a little "Canada sick" despite all the newness and the number of emotions crowding around me. However, dears, good night.

With all my love.

BILLY.

New Year's Eve, 1915.

Dear Mother,—

I've had no word from any of you, except the Christmas card from Auntie and the photo forwarded from St. John, for nearly two weeks. I got the photo O.K. It arrived the morning after Christmas and I am sure it is indeed a splendid one of "me own Maw." It surely did me good to look into the dear old face and I have it on the table where it is in full view all the time. I also got

A SUNNY SUBALTERN

the Christmas card Aunty sent and a nice tie from the G-girls. I had already sent them one of our Christmas cards. I also got a dilly box of eats from my little girl ———, a five-pound box of shortbread, about a pound of salted almonds "home brewed," a Christmas cake and two or three other kinds of eatings. She's a dear thoughtful kid and really seems to be awfully fond of me. You know (this is strictly confidential) I'm very fond of her, too, and somehow or other over here the thoughts of those that are near and dear, like you people at home, crowd around one in the evenings when there's not much to do, and tho' I'm not getting sentimental, nearly every night before I go to bed, I just quietly crash out into the night and look up at the stars and moon, and look over there, wondering what you all are doing. But anyway, dear, I am going to give you her address so that if, as may be, don't come back, you can write her, and I know you'll understand, dear.

Well, I spent one of the most rotten Christmases I ever did. There were nine of us marooned here, all the rest went away on leave, and we were elected to stay. It sure was a dismal hole. We just sat around all day, in fact I never left the mess except to see the men fed. *They* had a real meal, turkey, cauliflower, potatoes, soup, plum pudding, coffee. Of course our men are very well fed, much better than the British battalions, but it took eighty-nine fifteen-pound turkeys to feed them. However, to hark back, we "ossifers" spent a dickens of a day, and I sat lamenting upon the passing of the good old Christmas, like Dickens wrote about. You know everything is and was very glum—so many families in mourning—that I remarked that the days of Dickens had fled, surely, but I certainly tried to wish with Tiny Tim "A Merry

Christmas indeed, God bless us every one!"

Well, dinner has intervened and I've intended ever since being here to write you something about the country round about. It is Surrey and one of the oldest settled parts of England. Beautiful in the extreme, large areas of woody land with rolling hills and common land in great tracts. It also can lay claim to some antiquity. As I told you, we are only fifteen miles or so from Aldershot, but close at hand are the villages of Haslemere, Milford and Godalming. We were at the latter place which dates back, well, further than even I can remember, and feel sure that you'll agree when I say that I gazed with wonder on an oak which dates back to the Doomsday book in which it is mentioned. Ye gods, think of it! The other places are nearly as ancient, all being mentioned in a grant from my old pal, King Alfred, to his cousin somebody I've forgotten; however, as I never expect to meet him this side of eternity, we will pass along. We went through Haslemere the other day. Its town hall is 300 years old and I should have said that it really has no claim to age, as I read on a moss-covered slab that its charter only dated to 1180 something, in fact it is a mere youth, beardless and adolescent. My old red-headed friend, Queen Betty, once attended a fair there. It is famed as the residence of Tennyson, Conan Doyle, Mrs. Humphrey Ward and Lord Wolseley, so you see, dear, in all this bally land of hoary age, I feel like a chip on an ocean. The Portsmouth road we walk on every day started in the Roman days, and I expect many a Druid chanted weird words around a tree that sighs and groans just outside my window. Between here and Bramshot, seven miles, where all the Canucks are, is the Devil's Punch Bowl, a circular hollow where in

A SUNNY SUBALTERN

1786 a man was murdered. There is the ruin of the gibbet where they hanged the murderers, and I had a beer in the Red Lion Inn nearby, where they got the man drunk before the murder. Can you imagine that? Dickens wrote about the spot in Nicholas Nickleby where Nick and Smike walked from Portsmouth. Look it up.

Well, to-day we were "inspected" by General Steele. We lined up in a splashing rain-storm and stood at attention for about thirty minutes. I know that it was while Sherman was being inspected he made his famous epigram, "War is Hell!" The only bright spot was when the band struck up "O Canada." It's the first time it's been played since we left, and it surely sounded great. I'll add, at first; for after it continued to play it during the whole darn ceremony it sounded more like the Dead March or any other bally dirge than anything.

Gee! can you imagine listening to the strains of Lavalle's hymn while I gazed at a pile of red tiles, with aching legs and feet until they all melted into one, then honeycombed out again into regular cylinders. However, we're "a fine body of men." That is the stock phrase of every reviewing officer until I begin to believe "all men are liars." I know you would have liked to see your son in full war attire, full marching kit, blankets, extra shoes, shaving utensils, haversack, great coat, underwear, mess tin, rifle, 150 rounds of ammunition, revolver, binoculars,—I think that's all, just fifty-four pounds on "me noble torso," and I resembled the patient ass of burden more than ever before. Hurrah for the life of a soldier!

There is some talk of us leaving for Egypt early in February, although nobody knows anything, except those who won't tell. We are miles above the English battalions hereabouts in training, and can give them all cards and spades physically. Of course the cream of English manhood is already there, and there are just the remains, so it's not a fair comparison.

Well, dear, must close. Love to all, including —— who I hope is well. Papers come regularly, thanks.

BILLY.

IN CAMP,
January 9, 1916.

Dear Mother,—

I've just arrived back from a wonderful six days in London and that is the reason why you haven't heard before. On my arrival here there were two letters from you dated 12th and 19th December and I was very glad to get them. Also about thirty pounds worth more goods from that little girl in ——, including a cake, tinned goods, lobster, pork and beans, coffee, fruits, a whole box of spearmint gum, cigarettes, and an air pillow. Some girl, eh? However, I suppose you want to hear all about Lunnon.

Firstly, I can tell you that I can't describe it. I mean that adjectives won't come, and anyway thousands more clever than I, tho' not so handsome, have fallen down; but, dear, can you imagine the thrills that pulsed through me as I gazed on all the things and places that since boyhood I've read and dreamed of? Grey old London bristling with historic spots dear to every British boy's heart, I think, and doubly dear to mine because I loved history, whether by Green or Henty, whether garbed in fiction or just the plain red school book, and trebly dear because of Dickens. You know, Mother, there is something wells up in me nearly akin to a tear when I think about them all. Well, anyway I revelled for six days there and walked and saw everything I could. I spent a half day in the musty Old Tower, ransacked it from entrance gate to the keep of the White Tower, touched the spots where Anne Boleyn, Lady Jane Grey, Dudley, Mary Queen of Scots, and all the others lay and prayed and died. Climbed twelfth century stairways, trod twelfth century floorings, read inscriptions dug in the walls by prisoners, civil, political or religious, and came out in a daze, my memory flooded with emotions. Then Westminster Abbey —it is beyond me to tell you of the thoughts engendered as I stood in the vaulted old aisles, while a glorious golden throated choir of boys pealed out anthems to the crescendos and diminuendos of an organ the like of which I never knew existed, played by a hand that was guided by a heart and brain directed I'm sure by seraphs or cherubims. Dear, dear Mother, all through it ebbed and flowed the desire that *you* could have sat with me, and when the lilting cadences of a boy singing The Recessional melted into the peal of the organ I think I cried because you weren't there. You know, dear, I may never come back, but I'm so thankful for the memory of that wonderful service. That alone dwarfs the thought that I stood in the poets' corner, or that I walked where countless thousands have been thrilled before, or that above me hung tattered old colours echoing of the gone glory of some British regiment.

Then I walked miles in the old city around spots immortalized by Dickens, just started out and walked and walked. Of course I lost my way, but coppers were most obliging. I stood at noon in front of the Mansion House and The Bank and saw, I suppose, more traffic in a minute than those dear old legs of yours dodged in ten years, and I discovered why all these places are called circuses. They sure are full three-ring four-platform ones, each deserving of being the "Greatest Show on Earth." There is just as much to see as in Ringling Bros., and the difference seems to be there you look every way so as not to miss anything; on Piccadilly circus, for instance, you look every way so as not to get anything. I always felt certain that I'd have a hub smashed in and wonder now just how I escaped. I think the funniest sight I saw was a costermonger with a donkey like a minute and a cart like half a one, crossways on Trafalgar Square and the Strand one morning. A copper at one end shoved and talked while another pulled and talked, and every taxi and bus driver that was held up sat and talked, and as I'm an ossifer and presumably a gentleman, I really couldn't write you what they said or what the coster said back, but there were some fine examples of the "retort courteous" a la Anglais profanus.

Then we stayed up one night till four

and went at five to Covent Garden Market. That was a disappointment tho' as everything was dark, so we only heard the noise and smelled the smells. What, ho! that's sufficient.

I rode on top of a bus just for the experience, which was some, and looked down on humanity. Then we went to Whitehall and saw the guard changed. That is the only regiment not in khaki; the guards there still being in gold, red and tin plate. Being an officer I received a regulation salute. Ha! Ha!

We also gave Buckingham Palace the "once over" and went all through the Park. Buckingham looked very nice, but you know over it all are huge bomb nets for protection, which I guess spoiled the appearance. Then I did what everyone does, I guess, got lost in the Cecil Hotel, and sooner than ask I wandered into forty different rooms for fifteen minutes. Gee! that is some shack for size. I also learned that all the coal used to heat London went into a shute just outside my window at the Regent Palace hotel where I stayed. At least they started just after I got into bed and never even hesitated till I got up, the din being accompanied by raucous swear words and trite repartee from the navvies. The hotel, which is a new one, is some hotel, by the way, 1,030 rooms, and they had 2,100 guests for New Year's. It surely is the last word in hotels. A winter garden, lounge, a Louis XVI. room, a palm room, a grill and everything else you ever heard of and a lot no one ever did, and reasonable too, six shillings for bed and breakfast, a swell big room and fair breakfast, but never let it be said that London is cheap. I can attest that the idea is erroneous for it sure costs a pile of money to step around that city.

However, it is London at night that I should like to tell you of, if I can. You understand practically no lights are allowed. Stores, etc., pull down blinds and only a ray peeps out of doorways. There are no street lights save ghastly green ones that cause everyone to resemble an olive in complexion; and the busses and taxis creep along with no headlights, and even the side lamps, which must be oil, shrouded, so that for a poor pedestrian to cross a street is a dangerous undertaking. But to look up at the steely sky is the sight: Ribbons, seemingly miles long, shooting in every direction as bright as the brightest Northern lights, the anti-air craft searchlights. That is indeed a wonderful sight; the opaque little glimmers that surround one on the sidewalk, and those only on main streets; and up above, as one would think for miles these powerful searchlights sweeping across the sky; and then the slow-moving crowds, for they saunter leisurely along at all times; and the continuous nerve-

A SUNNY SUBALTERN

racking honk, honk, honk, of cars, punctuated by the shrill whistles of theatre and restaurant doorkeepers calling taxis, which are at a premium in the evening, all impressed me wonderfully. And then to step into the hotel rotundas from nearly abyssmal darkness and a veritable babel of harsh sounds —into a brilliantly lit rotunda, resonant with hearty laughter, male and female, encrusted as it were by orchestras, is some transition, I can assure you. To walk in and see the women gorgeously gowned, and the officers in khaki from the army, and naval blue and gold, one almost forgets that 150 miles away there is a war; until suddenly, direct from the trench, in walks a soldier, mud from toes to crown, begrimed and laden with heavy marching order, jostling his way up to the desk through the immaculate throng. That brings it back, as does also the sight of a poor fellow on crutches or without an arm, but it scarcely seems possible.

And what a study in character is there in a cosmopolitan crowd. Here a festive young lieutenant, there a florid faced naval man, yonder a paunchy Major, all endeavouring to thoroughly enjoy life for six days. And the women! Oh the women! Heretofore I had been under the impression that English women did not know how to dress, but the frumps we see are no criterion. "Lord lumme!" but they sure do dress. Radiant blondes in diaphanous garbs in greater numbers than I ever imagined, beautiful brunettes and sparkling sorrels in such profusion that it is staggering. They all loll around in the places irregardless of class. In the Carlton tea room one day a ravishing creature who turned out to be one of England's first beauties, sat rubbing backs nearly with a woman plainly a wanton, and I am told it is an every day occurrence. Anyway, they all sip tea or cocktails, smoke cigarettes and display an amount of silk encased leg to cause me to wonder considerably. And do you know I, in a measure, doubted my earliest beliefs in the decency of womanhood after some of the displays that I witnessed. Certainly a shock to my morals and mentality as heretofore constituted.

Now, my dear, must close, will write more later, but we have to welcome the Canadian Mechanical Transport who are just arriving.

Love to all.

BILLY.

LATER.

Well, dear, after reading this over I've found that I haven't told you anything; at least so it seems. I can't believe that my thoughts won't come for I always tried to tabulate everything that occur-

A SUNNY SUBALTERN

red so that I could tell you about it, and figured how to express it, but it seems as tho' I can't think of them. When I started this page I thought I could, but I can't. However, I certainly enjoyed my trip and the memory of it will linger long with me. I tried everywhere to buy something for Aunty and you. But somehow there seemed to be nothing for women, except ordinary things. Everyone sells war materials for men and the bally shops seem crammed with nothing but trench clothing, smokes, alcohol lamps, safety razors and steel mirrors. I wanted to get an antique for the house but searched, and searched, and found nothing I wanted that I could afford; so finally in desperation crashed into Harrod's and purchased you each a pair of gloves. The thoughts go with them even if they are only common place; you know that, dear ones. However, I did buy a leather frame for your picture. That was

A SUNNY SUBALTERN

selfishness, I suppose, but I did want to keep it nice and it was awfully expensive, the frame, nine shillings, but I'll just nip off somewhere else. Things cost like the devil here and food is awful. Our mess is something scandalous and I'm enclosing my last month's bill to let you see it. It is nearly $37.75 for twenty-eight days for food and some cigarettes, which is awful, you'll agree. We got our $100 here, but most of it is gone for a revolver and binoculars. These two sixty-five dollars alone—then a compass and several small things such as map case, fourteen shillings, etc., and I've yet got to buy several small matters for my kit.

Well, dear, will close again. Love and write soon.

BILLY.

A SUNNY SUBALTERN

ROYAL HUTS HOTEL,
January 31, 1916.

Dear Mother,—

I am only stopping here for an hour, and as I have just finished tea, I thought I would improve the shining hour, which has been a mighty scarce article for the last two weeks. My last epistle to you was, I think, dashed off on a typewriter at Bordon. Since then I've had an eventful career.

Dates are all messed up in my mind, but a week last Friday we left Bordon after two weeks of awful work and marched to Witley, twenty-one miles. Saturday morning, under orders, the whole battalion left for Bramshot, where we are now, and Sunday night I was, on fifteen minutes' notice, sent over to Aldershot to take an advanced signalling course. Some movement for your one and only, and if you were a Sherlock Holmes you would deduce that it presages something, and that something is, that we are to move to France as soon as we can be equipped, which is about the third week in February. Of course, dear, I know that that doesn't just appeal to you as strongly as it does to me, but it is really the best bit of news I ever wrote you, from my viewpoint; for, dear, it bespeaks much: first, that we are a well-disciplined and trained regiment; secondly, that we are physically fit to go; and when you consider that it was only in May last that we started and that there are 45,000 troops over here from Canada, and we with three others were selected to form a new Brigade in the Second Division, you'll understand that we are proud. Just think; we leave the —th, —th, —th, and all those others formed six months before us, behind, and so I say again that we, as a battalion, have reason to be proud. And you, as my dear, dear Mother, have also reason; not just because I'm in the

A SUNNY SUBALTERN

battalion, but because your only son was paid a great compliment. An Imperial Army Sergeant-Major from Aldershot who was in charge of the various platoons for some time, and one of those old-time regular army fellows to whom discipline is a god, told the Colonel that my platoon was the best disciplined one in the battalion and exceptionally smart; which is, you'll admit, a feather in my cap, and for which I was complimented by my Colonel. Then our Signalling Officer has been made Brigade Signaller, which is a boost for him, and one of our Majors is Acting Brigade Major, and likely to obtain the place permanently, and our Chaplain has been made Brigade Chaplain; all of which reflects great credit on our battalion, and we're trying awfully hard to live up to our reputation. Now, aren't you proud? One of Canada's premier battalions and your son a "hossifer" in it! I don't suppose, dear, that gazing adown the vista of years to the time of my babyhood you ever dreamed that I should one day stand where I am now. I suppose mothers like you can sing "I didn't raise my boy to be a soldier;" but since he is raised and is a soldier, I do want my mother to be proud of me. For, after all, dear, although I've never notched very deep heretofore, and, I know, not just accomplished what you'd have had me do, still I think that with your love for success, and the top of the ladder, you'll be proud that I'm at least a good lieutenant, for, oh, dear, I've tried very hard. And so we're going "over there," perhaps soon after you get this letter.

I want you at once to send me on a card, if possible, obtained from the Bank of Montreal, your signature, as I am going to make my bank account a joint one in both our names, either to draw cheques. This will enable you to draw out at any time anything to my credit, and avoid the expense of litigation or probate should they bump me off. Send the signature direct to the Bank as per enclosed cheque address and I'll arrange it here. Don't delay a day. The cheque you will keep so as to have it by you, to draw if you want to.

I am expressing back to Canada my rain coat, also my great coat or possibly only the latter. We all had to buy what they call trench coats, rubber coats, fleece lined, which cost seven pounds fifteen shillings, as a great coat is too heavy, and if it gets wet takes days to dry out, so I fear me is not much use. My other goods I'm putting in storage in London and will advise you in regard to them later. We are all busy buying trench necessities, such as high rubber boots, periscopes, Wolseley valises,—a contrivance holding blankets and clothes, as we are only allowed thirty-five pounds of baggage out-

A SUNNY SUBALTERN

side what we carry, and they must be in these valises. They cost four pounds, but are essential, otherwise you can't have anything taken. Suitcases and trunks are barred for obvious reasons. In fact, when I get all dolled up in heavy marching order which I described before, I resemble a Christmas tree that's been having a night out more than anything, and feel sure Richard III. was in somewhat a similar state when he uttered that very salient remark, "A horse, a horse, my kingdom, etc."

However, that doesn't explain why I am at the Royal Huts which I started to in the preamble. Well, last Sunday the Colonel suddenly walked into the mess and said, "You'll go to Aldershot to-night to take an advanced signalling course." I remonstrated that an advanced signalling was a trifle premature as I had never even had an elementary one, but old Tennyson knew whereof he spoke,

A SUNNY SUBALTERN

"There's not to reason why," etc., and so, like a lamb to Armour's, I hied me on my way.

Arrived, and the first thing Monday morning they just flung at me through space, six words a minute in Morse telegraph code on a delightful invention known as a buzzer, which is the same as a door bell run by a telegraph key. In view of the fact that I'd never even been introduced to one previously, and that I certainly wasn't on speaking terms with it, I failed to measure up, but I went to the Commandant of the School and between talking to him and crying at him, induced him to allow me to stay, insisting in right good Canadian fashion that as I'd come to take a signalling course, it was patent I could scarcely go home without one. I tell you that gift of gab is jake sometimes. So a sergeant was appointed to give me elementary instruction in the various forms of army communication, viz., buzzer, heliograph—a sort of Spanish-inquisition-looking-affair, which reflects the sun from a mirror across the country—a lamp with a shutter in front for sending at night, and also by wig-wagging a flag thusly from here over to there, and from this position over to this other one; a very simple little affair, figured out by some of the mightiest brains of all time, but requiring arms like the village blacksmith to send and eyes like a cat to read. Well, so far I've grubbed along, but you'll realize that to learn Morse on six different instruments in fourteen days is not just what in restaurant life is called a "short order." However, I'm working from 9 a.m. till 10 p.m. with three hours for lunch, the indispensable tea and dinner, and hope to acquire sufficient knowledge ere this week is out to pass out at six words a minute. So far, I'm just a conglomeration of churned-up dots and dashes, and find my-

A SUNNY SUBALTERN

self going to sleep saying dot—dot—dash—dash—damn—damn; which all doesn't explain why I'm here at Royal Huts. In fact, I'm beginning to question if I'll ever tell you, as I've just remembered that the —th battalion has been broken up, only a band and a few handy men left to clean up. Solomon said, "Pride goeth," etc.

Anyhow, to-day, being marooned at Aldershot, and wanting mail, etc., I came over to Bramshot, sixteen miles, and was starting back, or rather did start back. The mode of locomotion is a motor-bus which is a pay-as-you-enter-run-when-it-pleases affair. It resembles any street car I ever remember, inasmuch as it seats fourteen, but holds thirty-two. It seems to have a deal of trouble in breathing, and is rheumatic in every joint. I feel sure if its pedigree were looked into, it would have been sired by the first Ford and damned by everyone who ever rode in it. Well, we started out, the thirty-two all being present at roll call, each one a soldier (private) except his breath which was and still is and likely will be (from the ribald glee emitting from the bar) an admixture of gin and beer, (not at all like the fragrant rose of old England). This breath when breathed upon one in conjunction with a sweet scented odor of gasoline which leaks through the floor of the bus, only convinces me that I have nothing to fear from German gas. Well, anyway, we got thus far when the bus busted; at least she sat down figuratively, and no amount of coaxing would induce her to arise. So we jostled out and in here where I am sitting awaiting the arrival of another affair which I trust is more physically fit than the other was.

I have no more paper, this being some in my pocket, but must close anyway. Don't forget all the instructions and address always c/o Army P.O. Will write you more fully during the week, but want this to catch Canadian mail leaving Monday.

Love to all.

BILLY.

February 8, 1916.

Dear Mother,—

Your two letters written, one en route, the other from Toronto, arrived on the Canadian mail, and I was glad to hear that you arrived safely. I also got some letters last week at Aldershot telling me of the desperate cold. Gee, that was sure some cold, Eh! A letter also arrived from ——— last week and one to-day from ———. I am writing to her to thank for the sox, also to ——— for the cigarettes.

I arrived back here Sunday night from my signalling course and to-day received word that I got "Very good" out of a class of forty, which means I obtained over ninety per cent., and the Colonel is quite pleased and said to-night at mess, "Oh, I knew you'd pull through." Well, I landed back as I tell you and found that ———, my Company Commander, or O. C. Co'y, meaning Officer Commanding Company, was ill, and I was senior, so had to take charge yesterday and to-day of the whole company. That is, hold orderly room, which is the soldiers' court where he is punished for offences. For instance, John Smith in private life is John Smith; here he is No. 41144, Pte. Smith, John, and if he is wont to imbibe too much of the "cup that clears to-day of past regrets," is placed in the clink. The next day he is brought before his O. C. Co'y who, if he feels he can adjudicate upon the case, sentences him; but as his powers are limited, and if the case deserves greater punishing, he remands him to a higher court, viz.: the Colonel or Commanding Officer. Well, I had to adjudicate upon three yesterday and four to-day, all for being absent without leave, which is a crime in the army. By crime I mean not as generally interpreted, but anything for which he can be punished, and the longer I'm in this game the more I'm convinced that one can be punished for anything; and when a soldier is discharged after years' service without a crime on his record, I certainly consider him a mighty clever chap for covering up his crimes. It certainly is a supreme example of the two great classes, the convicted and the unconvicted; for if the aforesaid No. 41144, Pte. Smith, John, while standing on parade should be suddenly seized with a violent tickling of his throat, such as you allay by an application of jujube, and should spontaneously and ostentatiously burst forth into a loud "ahem," he can be very severely dealt with under section forty of the Army Act, the aforesaid cough "being prejudicial to good discipline." So you see that anyone can be shot at sunrise for blowing his nose. However, I carried on with the C. O. Co'y's work for two days, and of course being away first at Bordon then Aldershot was not in touch very well. Then we are being equipped to go to the front and are changing old things for new, and as the C. O. Co'y is responsible (not me) for everything, there is a lot of checking of figures. However, I am managing very well so far and haven't done anything I shouldn't have. Then to-day when I was in seeing the Major he told me I was to have No. 1 Platoon. That perhaps doesn't convey much to you, but it is just this: No. 1 platoon is the extreme right one when the battalion is in battle and therefore its flank is quite important. That is certainly a promotion, in its way I mean, for unless I was fitted to have command of it I wouldn't get it. It is quite an important spot and

A SUNNY SUBALTERN

D.S.O.'s are usually won there, altho' I'm not figuring on one. In answer to your enquiry as to whether all officers above me on the list were senior, "yes." But three officers above me are being left here, which makes me fourth senior lieutenant in the battalion. As for any notice in the —— papers, the place is about 200 souls, and anyway one battalion more or less dosen't matter very much here. A battalion is such an infinitesimal affair in this war, so I imagine the only place you'll ever find anything about us will be Canadian papers.

I was up in an aeroplane last week with the O. C. Headquarters Flight at the Royal Flying School, Aldershot, and enjoyed the experience very much. We went up about 2,000 feet and I imagine I should enjoy being an airman. There were no sensations except a violent desire to hang on, a sinking sensation at the stomach when we volplaned and a violent desire to get down where the air didn't bite one's face and chill you to the marrow. There was a slight rocking which tended to produce *mal de mer,* or I suppose I should *mal de air,* but when one is hopping along anywhere from fifty miles to eighty miles an hour you've really no time to be ill; in fact, all I did was to hang on, and just between you, me dear old Maw and myself, (and don't tell a soul) I wished most of the time that I'd never gone up. But then that is like the Catholic confessional, strictly confidential, and not to be mentioned to a soul.

I spent Saturday and Sunday in London en route from Aldershot and went in a pouring rain to Westminster Abbey. Oh, dear, there is something about that spot that really is the story of the Empire in a vest pocket edition that grips me. I sat Sunday in the north transept and heard the swelling (I think souls is the best word for they induce tears in me almost) souls of that glorious organ and listened to The Recessional. I heard them once again, sitting beside the monuments and statuary erected to Britain's heroes, and oh, do you know, dear, I felt the little wish creep in that some day my name might go down to posterity in those magnificent aisles. I was so close I could touch the statue, "Erected by the order of King and Parliament as a testimonial to William Pitt, Earl of Chatham, during whose administration, in the reigns of George II. and George III., Great Britain was exalted to a greater degree and glory than in any other period;" those, if memory serves aright, are the actual words of the inscription, and, as I say, unbidden came the desire that one day I might prove worthy of a wee small honour from my own native land, for, and to which, I am continually longing. It's all right to say it's cold, but then suddenly take away from one all the things that have surrounded you since childwood, suddenly remove all the environment that has encircled your very being and you cannot help but feel the lack. I miss the snow, the crunch, crunch of it under marching feet, the glisten of it in the sunshine and the glint of it under the arc lights at night. I miss the wind that stung the face and the cold that pulsated the blood, and most of all the air, the free, clean, sunshiny un-misty air of the west; and while I love England I wouldn't trade one day of Western Canadian climate with all its wintry rigours for a whole winter here. Tho' I sometimes cursed a winter there I now ask pardon and plead my ignorance as an excuse, for snow is immeasurably better than the same depth of gooey mud.

We expect to leave sometime between February twenty-third and March first, but will be in France for some time ere going actually into the mess, so don't figure I'm in it as soon as these dates occur.

You know, my dear, that its all very well to talk about writing to this one and that one, but I never get a chance to start a letter till 8.30 p.m., then its usually 10.30 before its finished, and I owe a dozen to different people. If I find time I'll write, but really some nights I'm so tired I can't, so they'll have to understand. Love to all.

BILLY.

February 13, 1916.

My Dear Mother,—

Your second letter written from Toronto reached me this morning. As I wrote you earlier in the week we are in the throes of departure and Sunday is no exception. Ten officers and a number of men have been away all day firing at the Rifle Ranges, and this morning in front

A SUNNY SUBALTERN

of our mess the Machine Gun class was busy rattling away. As I tell you, that's about all there is to think about. One grows so narrow-minded in this business unless you eat, sleep, breathe and perspire war, its ethics, science and the practical application of these, you might just as well quit, and our Colonel doesn't give one much chance to do anything but absorb warfare. As I told you, we are in the throes of departure, and I am told unofficially that the Brigade sails on the ——— for France. You will not of course receive this till after we've arrived there.

The weather here has improved quite noticeably lately. The days have been warm and bright, always for a few hours in the middle the sun coming out and caressing us and the landscape, so that it makes life a little more bearable. There is just a touch of spring in the air, the buds bursting on the trees, and this afternoon I saw several pussy willows and some snow drops out in bloom. Five of us went for a long horseback ride this afternoon, the first horse I've been on since I left the farm, and a rough gaited bird it was. She had a sort of self-starting six-cylinder action in her rear elevation and bumped along, also I bumped along with her greatly to the detriment, I fear, of certain portions of my anatomy, and I fear me also I'm going to be "rawther stiff" in the morning, as I certainly can class my middle parts as being sore right now. However, I enjoyed myself thoroughly for two or three hours, and laughed myself sick at one of the boys who doesn't ride very well, who had the wildest horse in the bunch and who certainly had a really rough time; for as soon as we started for home she refused to do anything but go, and of course all the rest of them also insisted, and when his bird heard the others behind, she legged it faster and faster. We crashed along for about seven miles through narrow lanes and tiny villages, and very Gilpin-like I can assure you. Dougal, the chap I speak of, lost his cap and none of us could turn our horses to get it. So as we must always pay for our good times, I fully expect to pay for mine to-morrow.

I had rather an unique experience the other day which I want to tell you about. Every one who hailed from this insular kingdom, in Canada was wont to complain in my ear of the slowness of barbers over there and always related how much faster the tonsorial artists of Britain pushed in your whiskers. I also have been told the same thing since my arrival and I've proven to myself the why and wherefore of it. Having to go up to London one day this week to the Record Office, I slept in and missed my usual shave before hiking three miles to the train, so upon my arrival there proceeded to buy a shave, something I haven't done for months, I nearly can say years. So seeing a sign, "Ladies and Gentlemen's Hair Dressing Saloon," I proceeded therein. Well, a bald-headed person of doubtful antecedents, judging from his physiognomy, motioned me into a chair. Not a white enamel becushioned one with a neck rest and numerous levers, but a plain red plush, one showing unmistakably that other thousands had sat on the same seat. It was just the same type as the C. P. R. or any R. R. in Canada issues to their hard worked station agents. Well, I sat me down, not without some misgivings, and, grasping "me noble countenance," he tilted my head rearward until I felt as tho' I were one of those contortionist acts at a vaudeville show. He smeared my face with lather and proceeded to scrape the protruding hairs off. I say scrape advisedly, for it was a process greatly resembling a man with a snow shovel removing the accumulation of last week's snow from the sidewalk. He didn't take long, I'll admit, and well he might do it in short time. Every time he let go of my head I endeavoured to raise it, but, someway, he always beat me to it and grabbed it again ere I could sufficiently stretch the muscles to erase the crick in it. He surely was active and I took a keen delight in seeing if I couldn't beat him to it. Albeit I must confess he came off best. Of course he was doing it every day and it was my first game and I didn't even have beginner's luck. Well, having removed some hair and the outer tissue of epidermis, he smeared a solution of nitric acid and chloride of lime and assisted me to elevate my head to a normal position, and, whisking off the apron, by gestures suggested I arise. I did so with face smarting and neck stiff and cricked beyond straightening, I felt sure. Upon a close examination which I made after a hurried exit and fervent prayer of thanksgiving, I found tiny tufts of whisker still there and decided that the reason they do it quicker is, first, because they don't do it, and, second, if they took any longer they would permanently dislocate their customers' necks; so I readily understand why there are fewer barber shops and why every Englishman always carries a set of razors. Anyway I certainly prefer mine own Gillette.

I've just paused a minute to listen to the mess gramophone blare out "The Veteran's Song." A glorious baritone sang it and as he came to the lines, "Thank God when the young lads falter we still have the brave old boys," I just wondered if, when the crucial moment came, I would falter. Of course, dear, I can't falter, there are no more old boys left and so we young lads must do our best. And oh, dear, while I know it's not in your heart I feel sure that you wouldn't want me to falter, and, somehow, on the eve of our departure we all have sobered down a bit. At first at the news everyone was gleeful, but we are quieter now. Things have assumed their right aspect. We all realize that it isn't a picnic we're setting out for and so we've adjusted our outlook and toned down our gaiety. Not noticeably, perhaps, to an outsider, but every now and then you'll find one or two sitting quietly and a wistful look in their eye. There isn't the laugh and the jest that for months has been usual, and so we go away over to France.

Now, my dear, there isn't much or in fact anything more to say, except I don't want you to worry. I know, Mother o' mine, that's a useless order to give you, but I surely mean it. You know we all are intending to come back and I grow every day more or less a fatalist. So don't worry, I'll come home one of these days and oh, how glad I'll be, dear, to fold you in my arms and hear you call me

Willie. So, dear, don't fear for me. Your God and mine whom I know you trust, is just as present there as in the quiet solitude of your bedroom, and if perchance He wills that I go out, well, dear, it's just one more sorrow heaped on your willing shoulders, one more pain to your silver locks. But as the days go on more and more forcibly is borne home the fact that up there beyond the Gates of Pearl there is one Omnipresent, and He will watch o'er me as he has done over millions of other sons.

Good bye, dearie. The last good bye for a time at least. I'll write you from France. Good bye and God bless and keep you safe for my return.

BILLY.

Love to all with heaps to Auntie and Uncle when you write.

A SUNNY SUBALTERN

We've left the lights of London
And the dreary rain of Hants,
For we're slowly steaming outward
"Over there" to France.

The while I watch the choppy waves
And taste the salty foam,
My thoughts are ever speeding
To Canada and Home.

I wonder, be there thought waves
Or static in the air
To shoot the thoughts I'm thinking
To my dear ones "Over there."

For "Over there" is two spots,
One is Flanders, damp and low,
While the other place is Canada,
My "Lady of the Snow."

And tho' my thoughts always are split
Betwixt the one and t'other,
I think to-night they're turning most
To Canada and Mother.

   Crossing the Channel as the lights of Folkstone died into black and Boulogne grew brighter..

BILLY.

A SUNNY SUBALTERN

SOMEWHERE,
February 26, 1916.

My Dear Mother,—

Well, we arrived "somewhere," and are billeted, some miles at the rear of the actual firing line where the boom of guns comes to us ever and anon. So we are actually in the ring side seats of the big fight and soon will, I suppose, be actually in the ring.

The trip here was very interesting, but I'm not allowed to mention anything about it so will have to tell you when I get back. However, I can tell you that I had my wish about the snow, for we landed in the midst of a soft melting snow storm which has kept up intermittently ever since. The whole country is covered about a foot thick with soft snow and the roads frozen hard, making walking and transport difficult. In fact, the weather has been very cold and almost like Canadian winter, as the cold seems to go clean through. However, the men and all of us are happy and that counts a lot. I've just thought all day what a complex thing is human nature. We arrived here, as I told you, in a blinding snow storm and after a twelve to fifteen mile march, finally got into the barns, where we are billeted, about eight o'clock at night, cold, horribly hungry and wet through, every man sore and grouchy, railing against the officers and any one else on whom he could vent his spleen. It wasn't an easy day and I, too, was dead tired, but next morning in the clear cold air we had changed completely. Everything looked rosy and in the midst of it all here and there a song or a cheery whistle, and after a good warm meal we were as chirpy as sparrows. Indeed, a contrast from the night before. Human nature is indeed a funny thing. I went out to-day to buy some woollen gloves and other things in a village about two miles away and I can assure you that National song of ours, "The Maple Leaf our Emblem *Dear,*" is just as fitting here as elsewhere. They sure soak one here for anything.

We are quartered in a farm house, the six company officers in one room of Flemish architecture—great oaken beams across the ceiling and a cold wind-swept brick floor and no heat. The men in the barns with plenty of straw are, I believe, fairly warm, at least I hope warmer than we are. The glass is out of our window and the wind "she's blow de herricane" across the floor, wafting in all the varied odours of the farm yard. However, it must be worse in the trenches and every cloud has its silver lining. But its some miserable in the morning, arising and shaving and washing at a pump with a foot of snow on the ground.

They say that to be a really good

fighter a man must feel a personal animosity against his adversary. Well, I feel certain that if old Kaiser Bill could suddenly appear some morning when I hop out of blankets and with goose flesh over "me noble frame," shiver and swear, he'd find in me a foeman worthy of his steel; and I think as the hardships (which really aren't so awfully hard) grow worse, we all acquire that spirit of animosity. The men, too, are not at all slow at expressing their opinion about the enemy, and they seem to be ready to fight, so I guess we will give a good account of ourselves.

Everything is strange and new over here. The very ground we walk on was the scene of fierce fighting early in the war. The fields, however, are all plowed and crops in, in fact "busy as usual" is the motto, pigs, cows, etc., chewing away, not even moving their ears. The buildings, however, bear mute testimony that there is a war on, and in the fields here and there are the remains of wire entanglements. I picked up a rusty old brass casing of a shell, while a few hundred yards away a tiny forest of crosses mark the graves of some English soldiers, and not far distant is a bog where, I'm told, the Princess Pats were first cut up a year ago.

It is all war over here. Every breath you draw seems to charge your blood with a desire to get into it, and its truly surprising how one actually feels no qualms about going into the trenches. So far I haven't felt the slightest tinge of fear, but of course I don't know exactly how I'll act when the crucial moment arrives; but I've practised control of myself in preparation for it and I guess that's about all it amounts to, self-control. Our first touch of the real thing was a hospital train we passed filled with the wounded and seeing motor ambulances flying along

A SUNNY SUBALTERN

the road to and from the firing line. Occasionally a stretcher with a bandaged figure on it, and once a body lying on the roadside, probably a real casualty. It's very hard writing, everyone is talking and I can't seem to collect my thoughts, also it is some cold. I'm using a lone candle so I think I've written enough. Excuse paper which is out of my message book and also the carbon copies, but I'm writing the same letter to the little girlie in———, and I know you'll excuse me. I'll try to write you a letter again as soon as possible and try to do so regularly.

Remember me to everyone and send love to the ———. Heaps of love and millions of thoughts of you and home.

Good bye.

BILLY.

SOMEWHERE,
February 28, 1916.

Dear Mother,—

Just a few lines to enclose some documents, one a joint agreement for the Bank which please forward direct, also receipt for goods stored at Thomas Cook & Sons. There is really nothing much there, and I cannot think it would be worth while to send for them from Canada, as there is nothing of any great value. However, here is the receipt.

Well, dear, the most important news I have to tell you is that we move up into the fight to-morrow and will be in the ring for a starter for ten days or so. Just to get our baptism of fire, as it were.

I received your two letters, the last dated 14th inst., and you seem worried *re* the Christmas parcel. I got it O.K. and acknowledged it the same day. I think, if memory serves me aright, the night before I went to London. In fact I'm sure it was that night, as I gave the letters to my man to post and will ask him *re* them. As for others, well, previous letters will have answered your queries.

I'm at present engaged in studying gas and how to combat it, and its very interesting work. I have to walk each morning about six miles, and this morning as I walked along I couldn't help thinking how peaceful everything looked. Bright, warm sunshine, glistening down on the snow, birds twittering, quaint old houses with cheery children running about and wee wisps of smoke curling out of the chimneys; in fact the landscape might have been a water colour of any country, so peaceful did it look. One would scarce believe that a short twelve to fifteen months ago this whole area was the scene of actual fighting, nor yet realize that less than a score of miles away the greatest battles of all time are being waged. Indeed, if it weren't for two things and you could suddenly transplant some one from a foreign land here, I feel sure it would be hard to convince them of their whereabouts. Two things, however, give away the ending to the story; first, ever and anon rumbles over the land the reverberations of the guns, sometimes short, staccato sounds, again long crashing rolls ending in a sort of roar, and then, on the pavé roads, a never ending line of transport waggons either bearing up munitions and coming back empty, or Red Cross motor ambulances going empty and coming back loaded. Nearly all the work is done by mechanical transport (motor lorries) which rattle and bump along at a great rate, spraying rather than splashing mud on you, while now and then a despatch rider clad in khaki oilskins hurtles by on a motor cycle, or a long line of the famous two-decker London busses, all painted war office grey, crawl along, sometimes loaded just as heavily as ever they were on the Strand or Regent St. But every passenger is now a non-paying one and there is no difference in style, all in "marching order." And speaking of marching order reminds me that I was in an "estaminet" or Cafe to-day, and there was a chubby gamin of about four marching to and fro with a water bottle and mess tin strung from his shoulders and over his left one a long poker, and would you believe me, as we entered he came to the "present" with his poker, then calmly strode back and forth as if on sentry go. And this almost within range of the big guns. The passive bearing and positive equanimity of these villagers also seem beyond one's ken. Business as usual is evidently their slogan and they certainly lose no opportunity to carry on any kind of bargain. As an example, the urchin, whose home is where we billet, appeared yesterday with one of our cap badges on,

A SUNNY SUBALTERN

and fearing mayhap that kleptomania was developing and feeling that keenly in one so young, I questioned him (for all the kids have a smattering of "Anglais") as to whence it came. Promptly came the answer "two eggs," "Eengleesh soldier," so you see the French are just as thrifty as ever. In fact, more so, I fancy, as every second house has been turned into one of these estaminets. It is possible to purchase anything eatable from packages of Quaker Oats to Heinz's Pork and Beans, and drinkable from beer to champagne, excluding spirits like whiskey or brandy. As far as eats are concerned no one needs anything staple anyway for we eat like fighting cocks. Meat, some fresh, some bully beef, bread or hard tack, potatoes and one other vegetable, bacon for breakfast, jam, tea, rice, cheese, condensed milk and plenty of it. The meat is usually beef, but alternated with mutton, and our Company Commander, who is an old

A SUNNY SUBALTERN

British army officer, says this is a picnic. Not knowing cannot say, but while there are some discomforts they are absolutely nothing to what I expected and we are all happy as kings. Of course I'm usually happy, but I find myself breaking into song every now and then just for sheer joy. That is, I suppose, a rather queer idea to any one who at a distance views the situation, but such is the case.

I cannot recall to memory all the queer things that have happened, as you may imagine, but it certainly is a very funny expedition. My French at the best is none too healthy, being rather pale and coming under the heading anaemic, so I've had some queer times making myself understood. In the first place through which we marched several gamins crowded along beside us crying "Beeskit, Beeskit," and I racked my brain for all French salutations and forms of greeting, but nothing seemed to fit, and finally a little older boy said "souveneer," and I tumbled. He wanted a biscuit like we eat. Hard tack, in other words. It may seem easy when it's spelled out, but when a dirty faced youngster grabs your thumb and adds his weight to the already enormous tonnage which you're carrying, your powers of understanding cease and your perspective rather clouds.

Well, my dear, I don't think there is much more to tell, but will write from our new quarters next week.

Love to all.

BILLY.

SOMEWHERE,
March 6, 1916.

Dear Mother,—

Your letter dated February 15 arrived to-day and finds me in hospital where I've been for five days. Nothing serious but a nasty attack of "toenail" poisoning from eating something too near the side of a tin. It occurred a week to-day, just before we moved down to Brigade reserve about two miles from the firing line. I had nothing to eat for two days, that is, could eat nothing, and suffered from acute diarrhœa and then did thirteen miles in marching order to here, which was more or less of a "via dolorosa" for me, and when I arrived was glad to lay me down in a dugout which leaked. Next morning the Colonel and Medical Officer insisted upon me going into hospital, much against my will, for the battalion moved up to the firing line, for its first time that night. It was a bitter disappointment to your "only only" for, dear, after one has laboured for months studying and instructing his men, and when the climax comes and all his work is to be put into actual practice, it comes hard to lie down and feel that he is not to have a part in it. However, here I am, hoping to get out to-day and go in the line for four days the day after to-morrow. I'm feeling much better, thank you, and considerably stronger. I think I would have been jake but for that march over the pavé roads which aggravated the case considerably. Of those roads more anon.

Well, dear, here we are, as I say, a scant two miles from the first line trenches and even here one is scarce able to realize that there is a war. For instance this morning, to look out of the window the sun is shining and birds singing. Here and there a touch of snow glistening amongst the green of the fields or fast being dyed by the mud of the roads, and not a sound of war penetrates the walls of the hospital. Except for khaki moving around from the window view nothing denotes war at all. Of course it is not always like that and there was a noisome bombardment the first few nights. In fact the first

A SUNNY SUBALTERN

night when I lay in the dugout it seemed to never cease. Battery after battery rumbled on and only a few hundred yards away one of the real big guns thundered occasionally. All this noise punctuating, as it were, the tinny notes of a piano grinding out a blare of ragtime from a Y.M.C.A. hut, the while motor trucks tattooed by on a road as it were beating time for the piano. Incongruous, well I should say so. It certainly, to one who hasn't seen it, must seem inexplicable. And yet it exists not only here as an isolated example but all up and down the line. How truly remarkable are modern conditions!

The hospital is run by a field ambulance and is a large building of four stories with a dozen smaller ones around it. Prior to the war it was a convent and school and still the patient nuns work here. Black robed and smiling they go about their duties looking after Belgian refugees, doing washing for the soldiers and running a small hospice where officers can get a meal. I haven't had one, but the boys tell me they are great. Fried chicken, cauliflower and pie. Pie I said. Imagine pie. To me that overshadows the fact that they serve with each meal a pint of champagne. Yes, there certainly is a high light over the pie. I care not what; custard, apple, lemon, raisin, mince, blueberry or cocoanut but, I could certainly cultivate a quarter section of pie right now. "Much better this morning, nurse!" The place has never been shelled and in the officers' ward with me, now, is a Colonel and a Major. The Colonel said he asked one of the nuns how it came that they had never been shelled. She pointed to the crucifix (an inevitable symbol in every room in every house that I've been in over here) and said "We're kept by the Grace of God," and I believe it. To think that for nineteen months in this maelstrom of war from every quarter, the buildings have never been hit and these quiet nuns have gone about tending sick and wounded, daily holding their matins and vespers, seems to me a modern miracle.

"O, woman! in our hours of ease,
Uncertain, coy, and hard to please,
When pain and anguish wring the brow
A ministering angel thou!—"

As I've lain here the force of those lines comes home more and more. You know I've always said a nurse had a halo around her head, well, here there's nothing but males, mere male orderlies, and oh, for the touch of woman's hand. I know that if there was a woman, were she princess or charwoman, that your beef tea would at least be warm and have salt in it, and there would be no sticky sediment in the bottom of the cup. That, and a hundred other things I could recount, betoken the lack

A SUNNY SUBALTERN

of the touch feminine. However, I've no desire to disparage the work of the dirty, clumsy hands which ministered unto me, for they are the boys who in their turn go up into the line and carry back the wounded. All honour to them! But that is just an insistent little fact that presses home quite poignantly.

After one has been a gay and festive subaltern in the C. E. F. for ten months one learns to do a weird yet fascinating occupation known as Map Reading. It consists of being able to trace one's way on an ordnance map by means of hieroglyphical marks and to know by the manner in which a road is shown whether it is a first class, or a second class, or a third class, or a fourth class road. Now, a first class road is supposed to be one, but I think that the first class roads here are the ones mentioned in the epigram or proverb, "The Road to hell, etc.;" at least they are hellish roads. They are all pavé roads and consist, first, of a line of Flemish poplars on each side. Tall and stately trees they are and from afar betoken a quiet shady highway, a *dolce far niente* effect, but, ye gods, what awful purgatory to walk between those lovely trees! These pavé roads consist of small blocks (cobble stones), and I have it for a fact from a respectable source that there was a clause in the contract which called that no two blocks be laid at the same height or angle in any space not exceeding ten metres in width by thirty metres in depth. So you can readily imagine that walking is anything but a pleasure. In fact, if I were a parish priest and my worthy confessees had hoofs like mine, I could think up no greater penance than to have them do five miles twice a day over these roads. Peas in your shoes and pavé roads rank side by side. In any event thirteen miles of them was too much for "me noble hoofs," which at present are blistered and sore. In fact any time after the first five miles I would willingly have walked on anything soft, Hampshire mud, a custard pie, six inches of snow or an eiderdown quilt. I certainly can never recommend a walking tour in France.

Well, dear, I can't tell you much about the trenches for I haven't been there but will doubtless have a few remarks about them next time.

Received the joint agreement and will forward it. You can tear up the one I sent you.

Love to all.

BILLY.

SOMEWHERE IN FRANCE,
March 17, 1916.

Dear Mother,—

Here I am again in hospital. It seems as tho' I never get out of the bally spot.

A SUNNY SUBALTERN

Nothing serious, you know, just crocked up with a deuce of a cold and a very sore heel. The heel comes from endeavouring to break in a new pair of shoes and started with a blister which, like Finney's Turnip, grew until the length, breadth and depth thereof was something to marvel at, and the pain in keeping with the dimensions. Talk about exquisite torture, but I sure feel that the methods of the Inquisition have nothing on this. However, she is fast healing up and we will go back to finish the breaking in of the new shoes. This breaking in stuff is no joke and I have not yet discovered whether it consists in moulding the boot to the shape of your foot or vice versa, but I think it is vice versa.

Well, my dear, I've already done a tour or two in the trenches and can assure you that they are the only experiences I've had that fail to live up to their reputation. Frankly, they were a keen disappointment to me in every respect, altho' I, perhaps, have not had sufficient time to properly sample them. There was mud and water to the prescribed quantities all right, but things are not so beastly uncomfortable and for forty-eight hours I never lay down or was even in a dugout owing to the crowded condition of the line. Of course one was wet and cold, but that's what we've been expecting, and the hardships are not, so far, nearly as great as I anticipated. Of course there was the danger of getting bumped off any time but altho' I'm sure at least two million shells and bullets sang, shrieked, roared, rattled, whistled (add here any adjective used by war correspondents, they all fit) hurtled by and around, none hit me. It was rather terrifying I'll admit, but somehow or other there was a distinct fascination about it. One's nerves certainly require to be constructed on the gyroscopic principle, however, to stand the strain. But the surprising thing was that despite all information *re* accuracy hardly one shell in ten does any damage. At least that was the impression I got, for none of my men were hit and the battalion up to the time I was brought here had no casualties after ten days in the front line. Of course I realized that perhaps the weather conditions were not as inclement as early in the winter, but still I really can see no such awful conditions as one pictured in their mind's eye. I talked in England to hundreds of men returned from the front, and by piecing together their garbled accounts, had a sort of patchwork quilt composition which I chose to call my conception of the trenches, a sort of pre-impression, but I guess either I was a bad artist or else the men I talked to were bad *raconteurs,* for I surely saw nothing like my conception when we finally reached the goal. While nothing is so bad that it might not be worse, and the same I suppose applies to things, good conditions in the firing line are neither so good they couldn't be better, nor yet so bad they couldn't be worse. Everything humanly possible is done for the comfort of the men, and every dugout has a brazier with charcoal and coke burning to get warm by, and there is food to spare. The meals are not of course served table d'hote, and finger bowls, I believe, even in the best battalions, have been reserved for future use; but eat you can, and a little management combined with the aid of a company cook, does wonders at getting a hot meal. Always granted that it is discouraging *in extremis,* also provocative of much blasphemy when George the cook is suddenly compelled to duck and use as a shield the dixie or pan on which rested your dinner. Because, despite all efforts of the A. S. C. and your own quartermaster sergeant, there is only so much for every one, and when yours has co-mingled with the soup lying underfoot it neither adds zest to your appetite nor yet improves the flavour of "Mulligan." Albeit this does not occur thrice a day and we usually are able to say inwardly, if not aloud, "For what we are about to receive."

Of course sleep is rather a minus quantity, particularly for officers, and it was doubly so with us, for I know I felt at times rather timid about the small sector of trench I was responsible for and wanted to be sure that nothing occurred. In any event we have not yet acquired the blasé air or nonchalant bearing that veterans of six months carry, so I say sleep was lacking in large chunks. I am now recharging the cells here, having lain dormant for two days, in fact hibernated, so to speak, despite the fact that out of doors it is beautiful weather.

Yes, I think that the "winter of our discontent" is gone for that laggard lover, Old Sol, has for two days wooed Mother Earth. And what an ardent affair! None of your brotherly pecks as kisses, but long warm Elinor Glynny ones, so that she is all dolled up in her spring sartorial effect. Violets, snowdrops and crocuses underfoot, bursting buds and the songs of mating birds over head, a blue filmy haze rising from the ground and every now and then a sleek grey Belgian hare scampering through the middle distance. That's the picture that limns itself on your brain as you walk along the road. Beauty, beauty everywhere, till one wishes one had the gift of a Turner to put on canvas the glories of this French land. I've just gloried in the view from my window here, trying to forget that the whole land is given over to war and that one or two high explosives could dint the landscape so badly as to mar it for sight-seeing purposes. It seems indeed a shame that so beautiful a part of the world should be warped out of all recognition. This hospital or rest station for officers is in a beautiful old Chateau placed on a small hill in a circular basin. Around the valley, as it were, runs a long arc of hills shutting off the view after five or six miles, but in between is really beyond my poor pen to describe. Wonderfully treed are the immediate grounds of the Chateau; Oak, Flemish poplar and several trees of unknown (at least to me) species, their tops gradually blending into one another till the bottom of the hill is reached, a sort of terraced lawn. Then the plain small farms with their cluster of buildings around them, tiny quadrangles and triangles hedged off with mounds of earth and sparse hedgerows where they grow their crops. Here and there a haystack or a terra cotta roof shows up, while the smoke from a village some three miles away, veers upward just as lazily as our smoke at home does on a lackadaisical day in spring. Everything over here, dear, seems to move so much slower than at home. For instance, every village has its church and spire, and every spire its chimes; and in place of clanging out with strident notes its quarters, half and hour, languorously the sounds float over in deep resonant waves. Long, long seconds seem to elapse between notes, in fact you count, say ten, and, knowing it's eleven, you figure you've missed one at the first, when "blong!" over comes the final sound. So also the windmills. I've read innumerable stories about the lazy Dutch mills, and here they are. Square, grey buildings with the regulation four arms that turn slowly and rather jerkily. They always seem to me as if a tired man were turning them at a windlass inside, and when the handle reached the top, he got a little more pressure on the downward stroke. I may have failed to give you the right idea, but it's here in my own brain. Well, I could go on telling you about this picturesque spot and describing the beauties of the surrounding country indefinitely, but better stop here.

As I tell you, we are quartered in this old Chateau—truly an old world place if one ever existed. Set upon this hill with magnificent grounds around, flower beds, rhododendron bushes, stately oaks, tall slim poplars, deciduous trees of every kind arching over long shaded walks which wind round and round, always coming back to the Chateau. These walks, lined with secluded spots and arbours, where perchance lurks an inviting rustic bench or maybe a stone or marble statue in a variety of subjects from Circe to Diana and Mercury to Cupid. Then snuggling in the side of the hill is a disused conservatory with hundreds of broken panes and a seemingly impossible number of flower pots whole or otherwise; and I could not help thinking of you and your watering can and a certain third story garden I know of. Anyway there are pots enough here that if filled would keep you watering from dawn to dark. Adjoining this is a very pretentious pheasant house all wired off in pens and walks and constructed of mortar, stone and wood like a Swiss Chalet, while stables and a most modern garage are further on. As for the house itself, a quaint old spot with high corniced ceilings and walls covered with tapestry. A large hall, dining room, lounge, salon and writing room elabortately decorated, and all connected by wide, high glass doors. Beautiful parquet floors of Spanish oak. The furniture is all old, very old, some of it Louis XIV. Old candelabra, antique brassware, etc., fill every corner, while paintings, whose value I know not, adorn the walls. And to offset this mediæval old spot, it is lighted with both gas and electricity and has lightning rods and steam heat.

Will write again next week. Love to all with heaps for you.

BILLY.

SOMEWHERE,
March 24, 1916.

Dear Mother,—

As you will see by the heading I'm at Somewhere. I believe you may have heard of this place, but I know that its importance is not known to you. Ask any school boy the principal city of France and he'll say Paris, but "Somewhere" has recently so increased in population that I believe it supersedes gay Paree in importance to-day. Of course it is young; less than two years ago it was all peaceful farming land but to-day it is a vast seething mass of humanity, its thoroughfares teem with motors, while o'er head fast flitting aeroplanes act as messengers. It is, indeed, the most prominent spot in the world to-day and gives promise. Desist, I prithee. It almost seems like the good old pre-war days when one sold or bought lots. However, dear, I to-day received your letters dated March 6 and 16th and was very glad to hear from you as usual. Mail day means a lot over here, you know. I also received another letter earlier in the week, the date of which I've forgotten, and I think a parcel you sent and some letters have gone astray. But they'll turn up; they always do. We've moved twice since they came, and I believe they were sent to hospital when I was there, but just as surely as fate they'll follow on for the Army P.O. is a wonderful institution and no matter where or when you move, within a few hours along comes your mail. For instance, yesterday we moved some miles and Canadian mail is due to-day. No matter where you are, along she comes.

Well, dear, as I say, a letter is always most welcome, for its the only link that forges the ends of "home" and "here" together. It's welcome whether it contains a lot of news or just a little, because really the alchemy of a dear one's handwriting causes all the dross of this war to sink, the golden memories of home, happier times, friends, and, best of all, love, to rise up; and then your letter was so newsy, dear, and what a coincidence, the dream I mean. By comparing dates I think you'll find I was lying in hospital when you dreamed and every few minutes over and around flew aeroplanes. So perchance there is something in telepathy even more than just a web o' dreams.

Well, dear one, I really don't know much to tell you, for actually news is mighty scarce. You see officers censor their own letters. That is, we seal them up and they are not liable to be censored at the base. We are put on our honour not to mention anything of importance, and it is left to our judgment what to tell; so really honour is a stricter censor than the much hated one at the base. However, we moved from billets up nearer the firing line and are four miles from the front line trenches, in huts which are more or less shelter-affairs. If one spoke about a shelter in Canada, I always associated with it at once the Salvation Army, or the Children's Aid Society, or a nearby doorway in a rainstorm. Here a shelter consists of some pieces of two and six surrounded by sacking, with perhaps a door. Of course it is very healthy in dry weather for all the air you get is filtered through the sacking. However, I told you that Old Sol was wooing Mother Earth. Well, publish it not in Gath, but they had a tiff last night and that hoary old beast Winter called in his (Sol's)

A SUNNY SUBALTERN

absence. The ground was about an inch deep in snow this morning and the atmosphere accordingly, and now there is once more six inches of mud on the roads; result being that she was "some chill-some" at six a.m. when you arose and tremblingly tucked your goose-fleshy legs into breeches and socks "dewy like the rose." *C'est la vie.*

I am sending you a photo of the little girlie, one of four she sent me. I don't mind telling you it is the worst of the bunch and really isn't much like her, but she is a dear thing, and I'm really not horribly sentimental. As for your being an in-law, I know you'll make just as good a one as you do a Maw. Anyway we'll try you out when I get back.

As for that code, my dear, if I'm taken prisoner there's not much you could do. I'm afraid Wilhelm wouldn't or couldn't do anything, and I presume I would be given the same treatment as the rest. Of course food is a necessity, I'm told, and Aunt Elizabeth could send bread and stuff over. However, if I am taken, which isn't likely, I'll misspell —— thus ——, if I think anything you could do through Cousin Jane would be any use, and if I do not receive the parcels sent, which by the way are a necessity, I'll misspell recieve or recieved by transposing ei to ie; both these will get by as natural, I should say, but there is a very strict censorship in regard to letters and they'll only let you write two a month, I am told.

We are in a part of the line now which is a trifle more lively than any we've been in before. You see over here the aspect of the war narrows down considerably. You are really only interested in your actual front, as it were, and usually have enough to do to look after that. What the Grand Duke Nicholas is doing, or whether Turkey has been carved, or why Manitoba voted dry, doesn't count. It's what is Fritz going to do next in this few yards of trench I'm responsible for, or I wonder if we'll move in or out to-morrow; and one has plenty to do to see the men fed and quartered and inspect their feet and rifles twice a day and see that they have their proper amount of ammunition and an emergency ration uneaten. You see an emergency ration consists of a pound of hard tack or biscuits, a small tin of tea and sugar and a tin of corn beef. Every man must always keep that, for it is against regulations to eat it except when in dire straits and on the orders of a Company Commander. But once in a while Tommy has a gnawing in his eight-cylinder self-starting 1916 model stomach. Then you see he has to report that "I've lost my iron ration, Sir." Of course you ask where, and he says that someone stole it, or the rats ran away with the works, or it fell in a well, or a starving aviator came down and stopped him, so out of the goodness of his heart he gave him the food. Almost any story made up on the instant goes. You berate him for being careless, knowing meanwhile he ate it, then proceed to apply through your Company Commander to the Colonel, thence the Quarter Master, who indents on the A. S. C. for another. Hurrah for the life of a soldier!

As I started to say, we narrow down our view here and a perusal of Canadian papers *re* the Canadian Corps can tell more every day than we know. Anyway the general opinion here seems to be that the war can't last much longer than, say, next fall. The Verdun affair means something and perhaps a few last gasps like that will see the tag end in sight. There is one thing I've always intended to confide in you since we arrived here, and that is I'm only another Henry Ford. As a Peacemaker I'm a frost pure and simple. I say this after unsuccessfully,

A SUNNY SUBALTERN

for many nights in succession, endeavouring to arrange for an eight hour armistice between my left hip and a board floor. I started out with the idea of a permanent peace; gradually felt I'd be satisfied with an amnesty; now an armistice is all I crave. There is one consolation, I'll never need a luxurious boudoir "Après la guerre" (you'll see my French is quite fluent, in fact I speak it just like a ——— Canadian). Albeit a disused dog kennel, an abused woodshed or even a dilapidated windmill (Canadian type), is a perfectly elegant spot in which to sleep. Ostermoors, homo-quinge beds or eiderdowns can be classed with Dodo or mastodons. Herewith a small Encyclopædia Soldierannica:—

Batman: a soldier paid by you to be absent when you want him.

Beer, Belgian: a liquid resembling beer British or beer American; evidently a distant branch of the same family.

Billet: and place so designated by a billeting officer.

Dugout: (*a*) men's, a patriotic dog kennel that enlisted, (*b*) officer's, a root cellar that got into society.

Duty: anything, everything.

Heaven: (*a*) Leave, (*b*) Rum, (*c*) Heat.

Hell: working party.

Home: a poignant memory relegated to the limbo of things unattainable.

Jam: a sticky substance invariably made of plums, used to smear bread.

M.T. (Mechanical Transport): a Juggernautical affair demanding three-fourths of the road and made to splash mud.

Projectile: see working party.

Rations: "Man wants but little here below."

Rum: a warming elixir issued in toothfuls by zealous officers.

Sausages: pork, a species of animal extinct.

Sock: an ever wet, sticky article, used as a covering for foot, hand or rifle.

Working party: hell.

Whiskey: well, the Governor of North Carolina said—

I really don't think there is any more to say this time.

Remember me to any one who would care to remember me, with love to —— and heaps for you.

BILLY.

April 5, 1916.

Dear Mother,—

Just a few lines. I've neglected you horribly this week, but work has pressed awfully. Saturday last, the battalion moved up into the trenches, and just before they left I was detailed to act as Transport Officer. That is, nightly to take up the rations to the men in addition to many other duties.

A SUNNY SUBALTERN

It is no sinecure, I can assure you, as it means cold blooded riding on a horse at the head of your transport column, seven limbers, at a walk, along roads subjected to high explosives, shrapnel and whizz bangs, in addition to being potted at by snipers when you get close to the trenches.

We go through one of the most famous ruined cities of Belgium each night, which they shell continuously, and also all along the way. We leave at dusk, go sixteen miles there and back, returning between twelve p.m. and two a.m., and I would like you to know all about it, but cannot spare time just now to write, but will to-morrow. A message has just come to say that the roads are being shelled more than ever to-night and we must proceed with twenty yards interval between limbers, that is to minimize the danger of the whole transport being blown up.

You see troops must be fed. No excuses go if rations don't come. If one way fails you must have another, and your brain amid the rumble of wheels and the rattle and shriek of shells, is always figuring a way out if one limber gets blown up. Personally I prefer the trenches. There, one has a rifle at least and the excitement and lust of retaliation helps. This business is deliberately slowly and precisely walking into an inferno—one that puts Dante's in the class of a skating rink. I had two horses injured last night and one man shot straight through his cap.

Anyway, dear, you and I are queer, psychically I mean. I've never had any odd premonitions, but to-night I feel a sense of foreboding, an impending danger, so scribble these lines.

Of course you realize, dear, that one schools oneself to dying if necessary. Not that life isn't very sweet but, when one is five seconds away from death for twenty-four hours a day, one grows rather careless, I suppose. However, dear, I feel that way to-night as I know I'm riding into it, so in case I get bumped off I wanted to write you.

All my love and all my thoughts.

BILLY.

I enclose a letter I've never finished I want you to have.

Dear Mother,—

Although it was only yesterday I wrote you the mood is on me to-night and I want to have a paper talk with you. You see, dear, there's something new come into my life and I just don't know how to cope with it. Although it's old, old, I guess it was old when Nineveh and Tyre flourished; yet right now in my own time, my own heart, it is very real and so I want to tell you about it.

A SUNNY SUBALTERN

You'll doubtless remember, dear, I spoke often within the last two years or so of having a home of my own. The ardent longing that ever and anon pressed upon me for something other than the vacuum of a room when night came on. It was always night when the desire came; night, when my thoughts, relieved from the duties of the day, spent their own time in rambling day dreams. Always with night-time came, I say, that insistent little wish for something beside a bar room, a club, a theatre, a gilded restaurant, or the four walls of a bedroom. Well, dear, I suppose that wish was the forerunner of the new something that has burst out into my days and nights. That something that I suppose must be called Love.

In retrospect to-night, I can not recall any event in my life of any importance that you didn't know about first. With the exception of a few boyish secrets that really cannot be considered, I fail to rake from memory's heap, one joy or sorrow that your mother's intuition didn't learn of or that I didn't tell you, and so, dear, I want to go to you to-night, my Mother Confessor.

Since I've really grown up and known my mind I don't think I've ever been what is popularly known as a ladies' man. I never had my nails manicured but once, and as a juggler of macaroons at afternoon teas I'm a decided frost. In fact, reduced down, I guess I failed to qualify in the opinion of the ladies. I am no Apollo, and as a matter of fact was too fond of my Ostermoor to arise early enough to titivate myself. Perhaps, largely because I had no incentive other than a desire to be only neatly dressed, I aroused in no woman more than a passing interest. I was always content to dance with them, take them to a theatre and home, with an occasional kiss surreptitiously stolen (I've flattered myself). Selfish perhaps, I made myself pleasant, or tried to, because it gave me pleasure to trot out a well dressed, good looking damsel. But when I left her, that ended it.

But now, away over here in war ridden Belgium, comes the grand desire for just one woman. It's a queer psychological fact, that every man in khaki wants a wife; witness the war weddings. I presume it's the old primordial instinct come out. He seems to want someone to leave behind; someone to fight for. He seems to want the sensation of the cave man, that of battling for one being, his woman. So, the natural supposition comes that it's one woman, my woman. At any rate constantly there is, before me, the vision of the face of the "Girl I left behind me." Queer little memories that come intruding into my mind, which should perhaps be employed in the weightier problem of figuring out how many tins of the inevitable plum jam my platoon should draw in to-night's rations, or some similar worry. But as I say, the memory of her intrudes in so many ways. Sometimes on a route march, as I swing along in the self-same monotonous step—for one gets to be an automaton at marching—the pictures of her come back. A picture of how she looked the first night I met her, of the profile of her, marked in memory's book at a movie, of sitting in the gleam of a grate fire, of the last weepy moments before the train left. All these and many more recur with insistent demand for my attention at queer times, and in queer places. I think that every night in that magic space of minutes that are one's *very own,* the fleeting seconds between the time I slide shiveringly into a blanket and the drowsy instant I fall asleep, comes the mental picture of her. And because that has always been a sort of sacred minute of mine own, a moment for my deepest thought, my sincerest resolutions, I feel sure that Love has come to me.

As I said before, the sensation is new—the longing for one person in all the world, so infinitely foreign heretofore—I can scarcely dissect my feelings, can really not comprehend it. Albeit, the desire for her is there, the heart-hunger for the sight of her, the wish to be beside her to-night, now, and ever. Ever the plans for a future home—that seems to be the goal of all the thoughts, no matter where the train of memory started, nor how tortuous the road; always the end is in the home I'll come back to, the home I've planned.

BILLY.

A SUNNY SUBALTERN

SOMEWHERE,
April 16, 1916.

Dear Mother,—

Your letters of March 20, 26, 29 all to hand. I received a parcel from Eaton's. Thanks very much. Also the parcels from Auntie —— for which I am going to write.

Well, my dear, I sent you a scribbled little note some days ago but you see everything is all right. The prescience of the future was a little strong that evening, I fear me, but I sure felt queer. As a matter of fact nothing could have been more quiet than that night. I guess I mustn't let my vivid imagination run riot any more. The nervous strain is absolutely too much, so will not do it again.

Well, dear, I'm still on this transport job, and I can assure you it will be somewhat of a relief to get off. You see you sit on a nervous horse and head a procession up to the ration dump. It's too bally cold blooded an affair for me. There one sits in calm majesty, as it were, and from the time you start out till you get within a few hundred yards of the trenches, Fritz heaves over H. E. shrapnel and whizz bangs—all very real forms of frightfulness. Then as one gets up to the line the road is peppered by indirect machine gun fire, and still one sits and takes it. You see there is no retaliation, —if one is on a front line trench, well, you could work off your superfluous hate by fifteen rounds rapid; or you know that by a telephone you can have your supporting battery heave a dozen or so onto the heads of the Huns, thereby proving to him you're asleep; but this old transport job is such a helpless, hopeless affair. It's as much the moral effect as anything, for, each time you start out, you know that somewhere along the road you're going to run into it and you bake that thought into a russet brown as it heats in the oven of your mind. You see Napoleon said an army moved on its stomach, and while movement these days is just a trifle different from his time, Tommy today has to have his beans, bully beef and jam, etc., just the same. There is no such word as can't in the bright lexicon of a subaltern, and I am thinking it applies even more to a transport officer, for no excuses are accepted if rations don't come. If you get a bump there's a sergeant, if both get it, a corporal, and finally a driver to every team, who'll do his duty and get the stuff there.

However, it is a wonderful experience to ride along a road that is being shelled. Perchance in the glory of a sunset, or in the light of the old moon, or yet again on a coal black night with rain making the roads like a banana peel on a granolithic sidewalk, and you as miserable as a human being can feel. It's wonderful, I say, to look into the hell of a big shell that bursts fifty feet away and of which you can feel the concussion. In fact, the longer I'm here the more wonderful this war seems. The psychology of the human element is most amazing. The other night as I rode up a road, above my head was the whish-whish-whish, *ad infinitum,* of machine gun fire, while on the ground the put-put-put of the same, or rather other guns; and, will you believe me, I found myself humming "Little Grey Home of the West." That sounds incredible but nevertheless it is absolutely a fact.

Well, Old Mumsie, I'd like to recount for you some of my impressions. For instance, can you imagine riding along a roadway, with the moon beneath a cloud and, from right to left, the light of thousands of flares going up; flares that make the white lights at Toronto Exhibition Fireworks seem like a candle, as against a 100 watt Mazda. As I say, flares radiating a pale white glow, guns booming, rifle fire cracking, and suddenly, out from the clouds, comes the moon, and there, beside the road, glistening in the light of Luna, is one of the small graveyards which punctuate the land. Perhaps fifty men have been "dumped"—that's the word—under those mounds, with the scant short liturgy of the service read over them; and you see the gleaming white wooden crosses like so many spectres standing out against the ground. "God's Acre," if ever there was one, not one acre, but thousands that forever and a day will be a lasting tribute to the manhood of the Empire. At one place along my route there is a tiny roadside shrine. It stands beside a road untouched, and sentinels the tiny white forest of crosses that loom out of the night.

That's but one picture limned in bold lines on my brain; there are dozens that I can't write of. But one is a ride in moonlight through a ruined city. Can you picture a city as large as, well, Brandon; a city noted for its wonderful Gothic architecture, absolutely razed—not a whole building left—here a wall, there a conglomeration of debris; a city of homes and stores deserted, save for a few soldiers who control traffic through its streets and who live like rats in a cellar? I know you couldn't picture it any more than my poor pen can write of it, but still I wonder if you can imagine the impression etched on my mind as I rode between those ruined walls while the moonlight sifted between crags of bricks and fantastic minarets of mortar.

I dismounted the other night and went into the ruins of a seventeenth century Cathedral, a glorious structure in its day, a world renowned spot; and there in the dusty debris of its chancel I stood and thought. Gone was the spell of sanctity that pervades one as he enters a consecrated place, gone the inimitable gothic work of its altar, gone the images of gold and porcelain, the gold lace of the altar cloth. Never again will the *Nunc Dimittis* be chanted, never the incense of swinging brazier scent the air, and never again will a black-robed priest from his latticed confessional box listen to the story of human frailties. It's hard to tell you, Mother o' mine, just the thoughts that came and went, hard to dissect the notes that sounded in my heart; but one that was as a clarion was the absence of a GOD. That may sound funny or sacrilegious, but it was the uppermost thought in my mind. Here a house of His wrecked until only a wall of broken stone and a statue of the Virgin stood to remember it by. Anyway, herewith a small piece of handmade lace dug from out the debris and presumably made by palefaced nuns as part of the altar cloth. I'll try and get some more for Auntie. Do not attempt to wash it. I also have some stained glass which I'll not be able to send yet.

Well, dear, its bedtime, which is a movable feast in this land, and one must grab as much as you can when you can.

Love to all.

BILLY.

FLANDERS,
April 27th, 1916.

My Dear Mother,—

I've been waiting every day for a letter from you, but so far it seems that there isn't one. It's over two weeks since one came, and every day I've put off writing, patiently waiting so that I could answer it.

There really isn't very much news to write you this time. The transport officer came back, so I return to my company to-night. The transport job was all right

A SUNNY SUBALTERN

but I'd just as soon go back to my platoon. However, the C. O. in turning over to the T. O. said I had done good work and he would remember it; also, he wouldn't remove me were it not for the fact that I was a senior sub. in the regiment. So tomorrow night up we go into the trenches, into a real delightful spot; at least delightful in the fact that Fritz makes it very warm there. Casualties have been quite heavy there lately. From the distance come the sounds of a band playing "Marching Through Georgia," and you know I've a sneaking wish I were. The bands out here are surely a great delight for, on an afternoon, from the four quarters come marches, waltzes, or overtures, punctuated by an occasional artillery prelude, and none too pleasantly obliterated by the strident skirl of the pibroch. Nevertheless the old adage that "Music hath charms" holds good out here and our savage breasts are soothed and our minds refreshed by the airs, be they martial or motherly, that every band sends out, from the famous Coldstreams, down to a cheeping fife and drum.

Humor out here is a saving grace and I can assure you there are lots of chances to acquire the grace. For instance, while passing through a certain town which has been, and is, continually shelled, a soldier on sentry duty in my hearing said "I was sent back to do base duty. This is a 'ell of a base." This caustic remark was made as he stopped the transport to inform me the road ahead was being shelled, and as we stopped Fritz lobbed over a couple of shrapnel just ahead some twenty yards. Of course no one who hasn't been out here can appreciate the story. You must know the setting ere the crux penetrates, but I rode along and laughed as much as if I were in Shea's and Al Jolson was "on."

But what I started to say was that the

most humorous humors we have are the home papers with their vivid descriptions, etc., gleaned by men who never go nearer to the front than where the rail head is, also the letters from budding officers in Canada. For instance, I read one the other day where a subaltern in ———, who is in charge of the recruiting of some battalion, said he certainly didn't think that anything could be so arduous. I'll bet if that guy knew how many laughs he handed a lot of us out here he'd feel qualified to start an act in vaudeville. I'll also bet that if half the gang in Canada who are breaking their necks to get commissions, realized the responsibilities entailed by a Sam Brown belt and two stars on their sleeves, they'd not be so anxious. Its jake swanking around Canada as a Major, but its different over here. One's responsibilities seem enormous, and really are, together with just the same discomforts and hard work that anyone on the front line goes through. Your men, while they are men and must not be treated as children, depend absolutely on you for their very being. You are a sort of last resort for everything in their lives, from clothes and food to seeing their effects go to their people after they are gone to the "Last Parade." You know, dear, I sometimes think it's pathetic the dependence of these chaps on me, and one only really realizes what a King's Commission means when you get out here.

I believe they've stopped publishing casualties by battalions or are going to, so now you'll never know whether we've been bumped or not.

I've not found time to write to anyone but you, lately, so you'll have to convey my love or regards, as the case may be, to everyone.

Heaps of love.

BILLY.

A SUNNY SUBALTERN

May 13, 1916.

Dear Mother,—

I have your letters of the 16th, 18th and 22nd of April, and altho' I've been out of the trenches for five days I've not been able to concentrate my thoughts on writing.

We spent eight days of veritable hell in a rotten part of the line, in fact the worst part I've ever been in. We occupied a series of holes, some connected and some isolated, ranging in distance from thirty to fifteen yards from Fritz's lines. They were old German trenches taken some time ago, and it is almost impossible to do any great amount of work on them.

Well, as I say, we spent the time in them, and I was heartily thankful to get out. I went through my first heavy bombardment at really close range. They dumped "Crumps," Coal Boxes, Shrapnel and Whizz-bangs to the number of about three hundred all around us for two hours and then attacked. Just as night overshadowed daylight and objects began to grow indistinct, one of my sentries reported a party out in the front. Suddenly from our right, rapid fire and machine guns opened up, and so I gave the order "fifteen rounds rapid." Keyed up and ready were the boys, and we gave them a few hundred capsules of steel. Squeals, grunts, and moans, then the reverberating roar of machine guns, and rifle fire ceased. So, our first real attack was repulsed. Further on, our line suffered more heavily but I guess we were fairly lucky. All the night they kept at us with bombs, rifle grenades and trench mortars to which we replied in kind vigorously, but they learned their lesson from that taut tense ten minutes. No more attacks.

That is, I suppose, a pretty tame story of a bombardment, an attack, its repulsion, but words fail me. The confines of expression are not competent to tell you much more. I've refrained from writing, hoping that in the interim some inspiration would come that would adequately convey to you a picture. I tried to dissect my emotions so that you might visualize, partially at least, what a day and a night —twenty-four hours in a front line trench mean; but I have failed dismally.

To begin with, the nervous strain is great, and when one has his heart broken in addition, it's hard to limn for another, the lines etched on your soul, the impressions registered in your memory.

My heart was broken, dear, because before this bombardment at all I lost eighteen men of my own platoon; eighteen of the best and truest fellows I've ever known; saw five of them die—one in my arms—all hit by these devils of Huns— hit by snipers who use explosive bullets— a bullet that tears a hole as large as a tomato can, and if it strikes anything hard bursts into three pieces, each the size of a quarter, that maims and wounds —a bullet that if it hits the head tears off the top.

God! I wonder if you could even imagine the primordial lust of battle that courses through one's brain, the desire to kill that permeates the muscle, the exhilaration that comes when you know you've actually hit one of your enemies.

I can candidly say there was no fear in me.

For months, in fact long ere we left old Canada, the fear I had that dominated my waking moments was not will I be afraid, but will I be able to control my fear. I was always afraid I would be afraid. Well, after the bombardment ceased I wasn't, and even during that two hours of mental torture I wasn't afraid, just nervous. But when I knew they were actually coming, ah! what exhilaration, what primeval bloody thoughts I had! A valiant desire came amid the fight to do all the damage I could, and I rushed from bay to bay of the sector of trench I commanded, exhorting my men to be steady and cursing them if they weren't, here grabbing an extra rifle and blazing its magazine full at the indistinct forms, or there firing one shot from my revolver. No fear, no thought of self; just the hope that we'd beat them off; just the thought constantly of what was best to do, how best to preserve every life in my charge—every life in my charge that was preserving my life. So you see, analyzed and tested down, the ancient self-preservation rule holds good.

But the aftermath—the vacuum at the stomach—the palpitating heart—the deep breaths you needed, that, if you did not take, it seemed as if you'd choke, the feeling you must sit down—the desire for a drink—the insatiable way in which you ate up cigarette after cigarette in long deep inhales—the hope they would not start bombarding again—the cheery voice you forced as you walked along a bath mat and jokingly curbed your own desire to shout by praising the men and belitting "the show;" all these when your emotions that had bubbled to the boiling point again simmered down. That night as I walked along and did my best to restore the steadiness of my men, ever and anon came those immortal lines of Kipling:

"If you can force your heart and nerve and sinew
To serve your turn, long after they are gone
And so hold on, when there is nothing in you
Except the Will, which says to them 'Hold on,'"

recurred again and again, and I offered up to the Almighty, He whose name a few minutes before I had taken in vain, a fervent, silent, little prayer, that I should be given the strength of will and body to keep it up.

Then the interminable night with every nerve and muscle strained in a long "stand to," with the added exertion of placing an additional platoon that came up as reinforcements, and the cramped, numb feeling as one sat in a narrow trench with the intermittent rattle of rifle fire, the insistent tattoo of a machine gun, or the hazy smoke of flares that ever and anon "swizzed" up here and there, lighting in their ghastly magnesium the faces of the men who, cramped and cold, waited for they knew not what. All these factors, I say, broke the nerve and strained the mentality.

And the wait for dawn. I sat and watched the sky star-studded, if ever it was, watched Ursus Major, Polaris, The Pleiades, Andromeda, a star I thought was Saturn, and one I knew was Mars—

A SUNNY SUBALTERN

Mars the God we're propitiating over here. I watched them and untold millions more fade into the steel vault that, by the alchemy of old Sol, melted into priscilla grey and imperceptibly changed to whitey blue, while rimming the East was the orange band that I knew some six hours later would herald the dawn of day to you in dear old Homeland. Then the real diurnal "stand to" as dawn comes up. Every man ready, alert and anxious, until bright daylight dispels all fears of an attack.

After that "stand down" and then Rum. Ah, that Rum! If some of those carping criers at home whose protests against Tommy getting his tot could sit with their feet numbed and chilled by eighteen inches of stinking water, could sit or stand for twenty-four hours a day in a cramped crouch and feel, as I have felt, that a chance to stretch their legs and arms would be a luxury rivalling the dearest wish that heretofore you'd ever had; I say, if some of those people at home could do these things, oh how I'd love to take them for an eight day tour, I feel sure they'd never open their mouths again. That mouthful of rum, about a half wine-glass, trickles down warming and burning, meanwhile restoring in a man whose nerves are like the lace on a window blind, a little vigour, a further lease on life, that in the grey dawn seems cheap at best. If they want to do away with their own drinks let them, but until they've been through the acid test of ninety-six hours without much rest, ninety-six hours of mental strain and physical exertion, mayhap ninety-six hours when every stitch of clothing has been wet through, please let them keep their hands off the question out here.

After that elixir, "Stand down!" when only the various sentries are left on duty all through the long day, but every man cleans his rifle and equipments, and if any water is available shaves, washes and tries to scrape some of the mud from his clothes. And then a breakfast. You who at home sit down to a half of a succulent grape-fruit or a sliced orange, with porridge and *cream* (I had almost forgotten that word), or a browned and sizzling omelet with thin, crisp toast and a cup of coffee, will never know what it is to boil water over a candle wrapped in sacking. The recipe for this is: Fold a piece of sacking, preferably dry, if available, around one and a half inches of waxed candle, place these ingredients wick-end up in an empty jam tin, which has been perforated with a knife; on this one places his mess tin full of water and lights the candle. Then comes in *President Wilson's* idea, "A watchful, waiting policy." Meanwhile, Fritz is sending *notes* in the form of shrapnel, which, while conciliatory, are nevertheless likely to cause a breach in your relations with the aforesaid can and candle, or even in your anatomy, if you are in its way. Well, after you've watched and waited and heaped on more fuel, which is obtained by cutting off the fat from your meagre slice of bacon, the water bubbles and actually boils. Then you add a handful of tea and sugar mixed by a thoughtful Quartermaster-sergeant, and the ambrosia is ready to serve. This with the unexpended portion of your extra fuel mentioned above, which is crisped in the same manner, forms your matutinal feast, at least, with the addition of your half loaf of bread which is held in your left hand, and eaten as a school boy does an apple.

I fear that this epistle grows weary, so will start with lots of little things. To begin with, I received a parcel of socks, candy, coffee and cream cheese from A.

A SUNNY SUBALTERN

S., for which I wrote a note, also sent a souvenir. I am sending —— a parcel which is for you, two nose caps off German shells and a bullet which clipped a piece out of my sleeve, afterwards burying itself in a good old sand bag.

Read the bottom of a Grape Nuts. Don't waste postage on newspapers and don't send anything except cakes, as we can buy here, more cheaply than you, fruits, etc. Canadian cigarettes always acceptable, also handerchiefs, cheapest obtainable, as we lose vast quantities.

Socks are jake, for if we can't use them ourselves we give them to the men.

Hope this bally "show" will be over in a short time. Yours,

BILLY.

P.S.—Later will send story of the poor chap who died in my arms.

B.

See page 168.

A SUNNY SUBALTERN

LONDON,
August 8, 1916.

My Dear Mother,—

I am going to try to put on paper, my dear, a few of the million pictures that are etched in the gallery of my memory. The picture I'm trying to pen for you is the one which comes to me here in hospital as I try to piece together the events leading up to the time that I got mine. I realize full well how difficult it is to describe "the front" to anyone who has never seen a trench, and I know if I'm not explicit sometimes you'll understand, I'm only doing my best. I fear me it will be a poor best at that, for so many, many times I've said that only a Dante could describe and Dorè paint it.

To begin with, you must understand that our brigade had been relieved at night after eight days of very trying times in which the Bosche put over about every kind of projectile he owns, from Minenwarfers or heavy trench mortars, to his delectable whizz bangs. He didn't fail even to present us with some of his famous "Silent Annies," a large calibre shell which makes practically no noise till it bursts. Well, as I say, we were relieved and finally in the grey "coolth" of dawn arrived in billets.

After some breakfast, we proceeded to go to bed, a most welcome thought. Off came the sticky clothes that for sixteen days—eight spent in reserve—had alternately been wet through with sweat and water, only to dry again; and after a few preliminary scratchings of sides and backs and shoulders, we dropped into the profound sleep that only weary men know about on that first morning in billets.

I don't suppose I'm any bigger coward than the average man, but I always felt fervently thankful after a tour in the line, when we arrived in billets. There, while not safe from long range guns, one could at least, relax, throw off the harassing strain, physical and mental, drop as like a cloak the responsibility incurred while actually on the firing line. So, I say, I, and I'm sure everyone else, was pleased with the thought that for some time, except for working parties, we were free. A "Thank God that's over!" feeling.

I was awakened by my man about ten a.m.—so blessed shave and wash—some more breakfast, and then we revelled in the thought of a bath. We went from hut to hut laughing and jesting, here comparing notes, there condoling with some chap who ordered us to "Get out, I didn't get in till 7.30," happy and free, little realizing what was going on a scant eight miles away. Always, always, there came the dull boom of guns, perhaps more marked than usual, but we jocularly said that the "morning hate" was a little worse, rather pitying the poor devils who were getting it. We didn't know whether it was the Huns or not, for our guns were speaking more than ordinarily. As we heard ours, up went that little wish one always had that those shells wouldn't be "duds," and the hope they would knock some of our dear enemy out. So, as I tell you, we passed an hour, when the word was brought to be ready to "move in an hour." Every man must pack his kit and not move from his own hut. Gone, of course, was the bath. We rather regretted that. We felt, I think, rather upset because we had looked forward to a rest, and I remember cursing the Bosche for starting his dirty work so soon.

Gathered in anxious little groups we awaited further word. After a couple of hours, we heard some rumoured reports that told only too well what we afterwards learned. Well, we "stood to" till sometime in the afternoon, I couldn't say just the hour for one loses all sense of time; then came the word to "move off."

Once more, with the slow step that is used on the road to the front line, we started. The first part of the journey was easy. Occasionally a lone shrapnel would burst on the road, but it was only when we got up into the area where the "heavies" were that we felt the force of the bombardment. Steadily we marched in the bright afternoon sun, here and there halting; at this corner turning off the main road into a by-way because the Germans were "searching" the road, until just at twilight tide we arrived, by devious by-paths, outside "Wipers."

The order was passed "no lights, no smoking, no noise." The last injunction was entirely superfluous, for between the shriek and boom of our shells, also theirs, coupled with the rumble of the artillery limbers that galloped up with more "iron rations," one could scarce be heard. Here we sat or sprawled in the dewy grass awaiting orders. Just as twilight faded into night, amid the roar of an exceptional burst of artillery, the sky lighted up by what seemed millions of "flares." The whole place was bathed in the ghastly magnesium white they cast about, the scene here and there being punctuated by a red or green rocket. It was indeed, I can assure you, one of the prettiest sights I've ever witnessed. The average pyrotechnic display pales considerably in comparison. This arc of light was continuous for some few minutes, mingled with the lurid yellow red burst of shrapnel. The colour of shrapnel bursting at night is hard to liken; it resembles more than anything a deep tiger lily which bloomed for an infinitesimal space, then melted into black oblivion.

So, as I say, we waited, as good soldiers always do, for orders. There wasn't much talking, in fact, I imagine that everyone was rather too busy with thoughts of Home. Somehow in the veriest thick of things, there's usually a thought of Home creeps into your mind. However, here and there a jest or a laugh came out. One man as I passed said to his mate—"Write to her." Some "her" who I suppose would have been thrice as excited as he, had she known. Occasionally, as a shell burst somewhere near, the inevitable question, "Where did that one go?" came out; but conversation was at a premium.

Just at the night of night, an hour before dawn, came the word to advance, and in extended order across shell-swept ground we started over an area pitted and potted by shells, with here a clump of scarred trees, or there a few gaunt stones, the remnant of a building. Everything is patterned in the Army by the Guards. To do things as they do is the aim of everyone, and while I've never seen them make an attack, I have walked along the same road under heavy shelling. Therefore I admire them. Albeit, I question if ever the Guards went forward more valiantly than did those civilian soldiery of ours. The Guards' line may perhaps have been straighter, but it could waver no less. The psychology of a soldier in the brief moments of an attack or counter-attack, is something beyond my ken. In retrospect, I come on the thought I had as I saw that line move forward: that line of *my* men, the men whom I worked over during months of training, the men, who with me, had laughed and laboured, cried and cursed for many moons, slowly advancing to we knew not what. A picture of a green sward in Canada months before came back, and I recollected my exhortations on keeping a line and steady pace. I conjured up also the visions of thousands in training who sweep over grassy slopes not cut by shell fire or devastated by warfare. I only tell you this

A SUNNY SUBALTERN

to show the queer kinks in my brain.

On we went in the gray of the early morning, past verdant stretches of fields, rank with ungarnered crops, which were besprinkled with scarlet poppies. We clambered through hedge-rows of hawthorn in bloom, the smell of which mingled with the sweet sickly odour of "lachrymators" or tear shells. We dodged shell holes or climbed in and over the remains of trenches, all the while drawing nearer, nearer the ceaseless rattle of musketry, the rhythmic rip of machine guns.

The order to fix bayonets passed along: this done, the clicking of bolts, to ensure that every magazine had its quota of cartridges, sounded. Over a little rise we came: just ahead was a line of lurid light and noise. Now, night was going and against the sky we showed up quite plainly, a long thin line of silhouettes, the lighter fawn of the bombers' aprons, each pocket bulging with its lemon-shaped grenade, distinctive from the others. So on toward the line of lurid light and noise we walked. They don't run nowadays; gone is the glory of the charge with its huzzas and flashing swords; it's slow and steady does it.

This doesn't take long to write but it was composed of minutes, each age-long; and looking at it now, I wonder how I, or anyone, got so far amid the pandemonium of bursting shells, siffling bullets and detonating bombs.

From somewhere, one of our officers rushed up and ordered me to retire to a certain spot about a half mile, as they, I mean higher command, had decided to postpone the counter-attack. Accordingly, back we started. Daylight with its turquoise sky had come and as we plodded back the Germans saw the irregular line. If before, we thought the bombardment heavy, now it was ten-fold, a tearing, roaring inferno as the Hun "searched and bracketed" the entire area in which our lines were. Shrapnel, whizz bangs, high explosives, hurtled and burst in nerve-shattering salvos. Everyone was mixed up, some men of another company with ours, also men of another battalion. We walked steadily on, until, the barrage becoming too hot, the order was given to take cover. Some few of us managed to crouch behind a hedgerow where, once a trench, was now a shambles. Here for the first time the really hell of the war came to me. That trench, or what was left of it, was congested with dead and dying. Men crawled along, over dead bodies distorted beyond only the ken of one who has been there. We lifted wounded men a little to one side while from each turn of the trench came the heart-rending, throaty sob of dying. Ghastly! well, I don't suppose there's a word been coined

A SUNNY SUBALTERN

in English to describe it. Meanwhile, shrapnel rained on its horrible hail, high explosive lifted sandbag and bodies house-high. Everywhere men lay half buried, gasping. Some, reason fled, climbed out only to be struck down a few yards away. And all this, kept up for what seemed aeons, but really was only about three hours. One chap, since dead, said to me, "I thought these devils were running short of shells. Well, I'd like to let some of those people at home feel this." Feel is the right word, for you "feel" a heavy bombardment. I care not how brave a man is, I say it reduces him to the consistency of a jelly fish. For after all, life *is* sweet and when one is a fraction of a second from the grave, he starts to ponder. Howbeit, the fire abated and we gathered together what few men we could. What regiment mattered not. Messengers were sent to report to the Colonel as to our position.

A SUNNY SUBALTERN

There were just three officers left of the company, so we held a council of war, and endeavoured to see to the wounded, sending out those slightly hurt, then sat down to wait.

Oh! What waiting it was! Expectantly, nervously, sitting while the time dragged on. After an hour or two had elapsed, one of the "runners" we had sent crawled back to say that the Colonel had been killed, he could find no other officers, and would we get him a drink—all in a breath. He was just a boy, eighteen I think, and the strain was too much for him. He was completely unstrung, for, after awhile, he laughed rather hysterically and babbled incoherently. Suddenly he jumped up, climbed into the open, his sole thought to get away; but there, a scant hundred yards, we saw him fall. He had found quiet and peace all right. After a time one of the boys crawled out to find him dead.

Gradually, as the morning wore on, limping or crawling men came up to report themselves. Men of other units, men of our own, and one poor chap, quite insane, who insisted that one of the officers was his brother. Up above, aeroplanes purred, as, glinting in the sunlight, they kept off the enemy machines, whose object would have been to discover the position of ourselves and other reinforcements. I sat and looked at a little triangular lake shimmering in the distance, and longed for some fish. I recollect resolving that when I got leave, the first meal in England would be fish. Looking back, I cannot remember that I ever doubted I would get leave, the idea never struck me that I might go on "The Long Leave." So is the human brain constituted.

Regularly, at intervals all morning, the area was shelled by the Germans. Starting in one place they systematically blasted almost every square yard of the ground, and each time seemed to be worse than the former ones; tho' God knows anyone was a cataclysm.

The day wore on. In mid-afternoon came word to proceed to —— there to counter-attack a certain part of the line. We gathered together the men, some eighty that were immediately at hand, and started off. It was a trip practically in the open as any trenches had been so battered as to be useless. From every direction came long files of men, all centralizing along a given line. I can't remember the exact time the thing was planned for, but we started off. Of course so did the artillery. Ours opened up, and if we got unutterable hell before so did the Germans now. However, *they* still had some ammunition, and the shells burst there—and there—and there—and then—

A SUNNY SUBALTERN

A drink of water;
A scarlet cross fronting a vision in blue and white;
Cool deft hands;
White sheets;
The throb of a motor;
The swirl of water;
The tiny toot of an English engine;
Another motor;
A bunch of roses mixed up with eye-glasses and perfume;
A *white* handkerchief;
A few jolts;
A bed;
Familiar street noises with the dawning realization of a hospital in Blighty, dear old London at last.

That's the best way I can tell you. I'm enclosing a couple of pictures of the Red House. Will write again this week.

Yours,

BILLY.

A SUNNY SUBALTERN

Moriturus Te Salutat

McCarthy was his name. On his attestation paper was the statement that he was a chef, and in the C. E. F. he was usually to be found in the cook house. The chef of even a second-rate hotel would have blushed had one linked his name with Mac's, for I presume that he, McCarthy, in his entire life had never handled "hors d'oeuvre varies," or that "boeuf froid" suggested to him anything but a joint of red and yellow roasted yesterday. No, Mac knew nothing of table d'hote meals or French pastry. His cooking was of the kind known as Mulligan, and a rattling good Mulligan he made. I've stood and watched him many a day last summer, as under the canvas cook house of a camp in Canada, he diced onions with a butcher knife, non-chalantly stirring boiling rice with the same knife —a perfunctory wipe on an erstwhile white apron being as it were the "entr'acte." In fact, Mac's culinary abilities had been fostered in camps not military, but lumbering and construction. His was an art that could set a pot of beans to soak yesterday, and to-night, for 200 men, turn out a dish of "pork and" so tempting that I was often wont to ask for a plate of them myself. He also turned out porridge in such quantities as to stagger one who had never watched a hungry hundred, fresh from one hour's physical line up for their morning feast. What boots it if there were lumps or if perhaps one got a small ladle full that could have stood another quarter hour cooking; it filled up that insatiable maw of a man in training.

Such a cook was McCarthy, but he

A SUNNY SUBALTERN

shone in another sphere with even greater brilliance than that of the cook house. That was as a comedian.

His assets were cooking and comedy, and when Generals and things came round to "suspect" our battalion, all ranks being on parade, these attributes did not redound particularly to the glory of the pageant. For McCarthy never learned to "present" a Ross Mark III in three motions. Whether he carried his comedy onto the parade ground of Generals, or whether it was because his hands were more adept with a chef's knife than a rifle, I'll not judge; but his "present," done in manner similar to the way he stirred the rice, always spoiled the effect, and I've often cursed him to myself when hearing a movement behind me after all was quiet, knew McCarthy to be still "presenting arms."

However, forgotten were these little faults when, just after reveille on orderly dog duty, one walked into the kitchens and McCarthy was the first to say—"Good morning, Sir; it's a trifle cold this morning. Will you have a cup of coffee?" I can't say about the other chaps, but I always did, and as one overlooked the kitchens, inquiring from the Sergeant cook if things were under way or the rations all right, McCarthy usually produced a crisp, hot-buttered slice of brown toast. So, for these, we forgave those.

But as I say, far above his cooking was his comedy. A master in the art of repartee, of his kind, he never failed to have a jest ready when the chance came; or if the Y. M. C. A. man got up a concert, McCarthy was sure to be there, either headlining or as an added attraction. His was the comedy that on the fields of Flanders "bucks up" a whole company, nay a battalion, as some merry quip just made is laughingly told from bay to bay,

A SUNNY SUBALTERN

so that in the midst of shelling a laugh infectious and hearty rings as a tocsin.

I couldn't tell you all the merry words he uttered—all the good-natured banter he gave between the day he 'listed and the day he died. And that reminds me, I must to my muttons.

It was just at "stand down" one morning last May—a beautiful morn it was I remember. The grass was green and the shrapnel-scarred trees were trying to burst out into a few sparse leaves. A hawthorn bush or two just to the rear of the trench was white with bloom, as Maeterlinck says "Yielding up its soul in perfume" distinctly noticeable even among the varied smells of the trench. In the distance, over from the Bosche trenches, one heard the plaintive triple cry of a cuckoo, that hoohoo, hoohoo, hoo-hooed every morning. Here and there a swallow flitted and dove in the first smile of old Sol rimming the tree tops to the east, and all was still, as still as that first hour of dawn on the Front can be, sometimes.

I remember it well and thought how ominous it was, and as I walked with a once full rum jar along bay and traverse, I pondered upon the stillness. I came to the bay where McCarthy was on duty. Alone he stood, lazily cleaning his rifle, meanwhile watching a mess tin of water heating over a candle. He looked at the rum jar and laughingly asked if he couldn't have his ration, knowing full well that I knew he'd had it; when with a dull boom from the east came the herald announcing the morning hate. I passed on, was in the traverse, when, hearing the sough of a shell, I turned. There stood McCarthy, rifle in hand, face turned to the azure above and in his loudest tones, addressed the screaming shell with "Good morning Fritz."

I heard him say it as plainly, as at the

same instant I heard it burst almost directly overhead. Its pall of black smoke hovered there, while its rain of death descended with the peculiar indescribable whine of shrapnel. It caromed off my tin hat, it smashed the rum charge in my hand, it ripped sand bag and tore corrugated iron, but, as they say, "It didn't have my number on it." One of the freaks of shell fire. It left me, but took McCarthy.

I turned and saw him slowly sink clutching at his tunic. I sent an inquiring individual, whose head popped out of a dugout close by, for the stretcher-bearer, and with a man who came moved McCarthy to another bay. There he lay as I cut off his tunic, his shirt, only to find his breast and shoulders peppered as a colander. Just over his heart was a huge ragged hole, from which the red arterial blood pulsed slowly in great jets. He was gone—I knew that—but I forced a quarter grain of morphia between the blood-flecked lips.

The stretcher-bearers came, but McCarthy needed no shell dressings, no iodine capsule. The ashy gray of his face, the wild stare of his eye, the convulsive clutch of his hand betokened that the strange metamorphosis known as Death was silently creeping nigh.

I gave him a cup of water. As I lowered his head a wan smile lit his countenance and he weakly said—"Do you remember, Sir, the night you said 'Gunga Din?' Well, that's how the water tastes." And then to some of the boys who had gathered, he turned, "No more Mulligan, boys." And with the same smile to me, "It's funny, Sir, how I spoke to that shell. It ain't often one calls their own number."

Which was how McCarthy, cook-comedian, in his own way, said
        Moriturus Te Salutat.

CPSIA information can be obtained
at www.ICGtesting.com
Printed in the USA
BVHW030847050919
557653BV00001B/20/P